DUNCAN LONG

MODERN BALLISTIC ARMOR

CLOTHING, BOMB BLANKETS, SHIELDS, VEHICLE PROTECTION...

EVERYTHING YOU NEED TO KNOW

PALADIN PRESS
BOULDER, COLORADO

MODERN BALLISTIC ARMOR

Also by Duncan Long:

AK47: The Complete Kalashnikov Family of Assault Rifles
AR-7 Super Systems
The AR-15/M16: A Practical Guide
AR-15/M16 Super Systems
Automatics: Fast Firepower, Tactical Superiority
Combat Ammunition: Everything You Need to Know
Combat Revolvers: The Best (and Worst) Modern Wheelguns
Combat Rifles of the 21st Century: Futuristic Firearms for Tomorrow's Battlefields
Making Your AR-15 into a Legal Pistol
The Mini-14: The Plinker, Hunter, Assault, and Everything Else Rifle
Mini-14 Super Systems
Modern Sniper Rifles
Powerhouse Pistols: The Colt 1911 and Browning Hi-Power Sourcebook
The Ruger .22 Automatic Pistol: Standard/Mark I/Mark II Series
Streetsweepers: The Complete Book of Combat Shotguns
The Sturm, Ruger 10/22 Rifle and .44 Magnum Carbine
The Terrifying Three: Uzi, Ingram, and Intratec Weapons Families

Modern Ballistic Armor: Clothing, Bomb Blankets, Shields, Vehicle Protection . . . Everything You Need to Know
by Duncan Long

ISBN 0-87364-391-7
Printed in the United States of America

Published by Paladin Press, a division of
Paladin Enterprises, Inc., P.O. Box 1307,
Boulder, Colorado 80306, USA.
(303) 443-7250

Direct inquiries and/or orders to the above address.

Front cover photograph: courtesy of Second Chance Body Armor, Inc.
Rear cover photograph: courtesy of Second Chance Body Armor, Inc.

Contents

Warning

Technical data is presented here, particularly technical data on effectiveness of vests in stopping bullets or other projectiles. The use of ballistic armor inevitably reflects the author's individual beliefs and experience with particular equipment and components under specific circumstances which the reader cannot duplicate exactly. The information in this book should therefore be used for guidance only and approached with great caution. Neither the author nor the publisher assumes any responsibility for the use or misuse of the information contained in this book.

Introduction

Ever since the first caveman bashed someone on the side of the head with a club, fighters have dreamed of being impervious to the weapons of their opponents. During brief periods of time, defensive shields and armor have allowed such dreams to come true.

Such dreams come true for only brief periods, however, for the history of warfare is a history of developing technologies. New technologies and materials are quickly adapted to warfare wherever possible and armor which is effective one day soon becomes obsolete.

The first successful piece of armor was the shield. Dating back to prehistoric times, the shield was probably first made from wood and animal hides. Flint and metal weapons gradually defeated such armor, which was replaced—over thousands of years—by thicker and stronger materials. As metallurgy developed, bronze and iron plate shields appeared on the battlefield.

Body armor was a logical successor to the shield. Helmets and breastplates were probably first used to augment the shield with new bits of armor being added over time in the form of visors, greaves, etc. Full suits of armor and chain mail were to be seen in the Middle Ages.

As weapons developed more ballistic velocity, metal armor became thicker and heavier. Toward the end of the twelfth century, knights were almost entirely encased in armor. This "evolution" of armor continued with the breeding of larger horses and the development of saddles and stirrups to hold knights in place.

By the mid-fourteenth century, a knight's armor created a heavy load. Mounted knights wore the following armor: a mail shirt (hauberk) with metal plates strapped to its sleeves: chain mail covers over the crotch and upper legs; a helmet (with interior padding) and visor; plate armor over the legs; jointed armor shoes (sabatons); jointed armor gauntlets; breast- and backplates; a heavily padded cloth surcoat; and a shield which allowed the knight to augment his protection at points of attack.

This armor weighed two hundred or more pounds; knights in armor had to be hoisted into their saddles. In some battles, more knights died from suffocation in the mud of the battlefield than from wounds since, when they fell from their horses, the weight of the armor made it impossible for them to get up.

The declining use of medieval armor anticipated the European Renaissance. It wasn't brought about by gunpowder weapons—as is often thought—but rather by the crossbow, longbow, and pike.

The crossbow and longbow—especially at close ranges and with steel arrowheads—developed enough energy to penetrate a knight's armor. Although crossbows were outlawed for a time to keep peasants from getting the upper hand with nobility, it didn't take long for the new weapons to turn up on the battlefield. Likewise, the pike, when used by groups of men, allowed an individual to strike beyond the reach of a knight on horseback and easily bring down the knight's horse, making short work of the knight himself.

A third "invention," the small dagger, was capable of reaching between the steel plates of a fallen knight's armor and inflicting the coup de grace.

Because a suited knight was a large expenditure compared to a man with bow and arrows or pike, economics dictated the demise of the knight. Though helmets, breastplates, and chain mail continued to be used for some time, full suits of armor quickly became but decorative items for the hallways of castles.

Pieces of armor continued to be used to deflect low-velocity projectiles, which became more of a problem as cannons were introduced to battle. Thus, the steel helmet and sometimes the breastplate were to be seen in the battle long after other pieces of armor had vanished. The helmet itself continues to be used, and there is little reason to think that it won't make the transition on into the twenty-first century's battlefields.

During the late 1800s and into the next century, bullet design more or less stabilized for small arms, and inventors concentrated on perfecting firearm propellants and firearms rather than bullets. At this point, armor again caught up as new steel alloys and plastic fibers were developed which could actually stop low-velocity pistol bullets or shrapnel. The most successful of these were introduced as flak jackets by the United States on a trial basis in the Korean War. These jackets often failed to protect wearers from bullets. They did sometimes produce miraculous results, though, when GIs dived onto grenades to protect their comrades and to their surprise, they got up unharmed because of the protection of the ballistic vest.

As riots and powerful firearms have started to be encountered more frequently by the police, police departments have started using various types of plastic armor, including ballistic helmets, shields, and vests. While these are not capable of stopping high-powered rifle bullets, they generally prove more than adequate for most street encounters.

Likewise, with terrorism spreading, dignitaries and bodyguards have started using ballistic materials, often disguised as articles of clothing, to defeat the bullets fired at them in surprise attacks.

As riots and powerful firearms were encountered more frequently by police in the 1960s and 70s, police departments started using various types of plastic armor, including ballistic helmets, shields and vests. These devices have greatly reduced the injuries that might otherwise have been suffered by those in the law-enforcement community. Shown is the "Command Jac" from Second Chance. Photo courtesy of Second Chance Body Armor, Inc.

Terrorism has also caused armor originally developed for military vehicles (such as tanks and personnel carriers) to become popular on the civilian market in the form of armored cars and armor plates for banks and other business buildings, along with "bulletproof" glass and plastics.

As the new armor has been introduced, a new race has commenced to develop new types of armor-piercing bullets. Likewise, the new types of composite material armor are being created to stop such bullets. Mixed into this race are new offensive tactics whose objective is to injure areas of an opponent's body not protected by armor and the introduction of new types of weapons—including "new" daggers—capable of defeating new body armor. These daggers are not unlike those developed during the Middle Ages to pierce the knight's armor.

Where will it end?

No one is certain, but there currently seems to be a trend toward multiple pieces of body armor. This is especially evident in Japan where police often face brutal hand-to-hand fighting against rioters. Helmets which nearly encase the head and armor for the chest and arms are often seen on Japanese policemen. Likewise, the United States marketplace offers shields, full head shrouds, ballistic gloves, and visors to create an increasingly knight-like outfit. The race may well end with all combatants wearing Star Wars-style plastic armor.

1: Materials

During the late 1800s, some experimentation was done using hardened steel plates to stop lead bullets. Probably the most notable of these was the work done by a German tailor, Herr Dowe, who in 1894 developed a metal breastplate which was capable of stopping the rifle bullets of the day. Although the German Army showed some interest in the armor, little if any of such armor was ever actually used in battle, and the new armor did all its work in the form of exhibitions and demonstrations.

The first modern use of body armor, except for the steel helmet, was by United States troops in the Korean War. This armor was formed from laminated fiberglass and resin plates which were placed into heavily padded vests. Later, ballistic nylon was woven into "flak jackets" by the U.S. military and saw extensive use in Vietnam, where it reduced the injuries created by shrapnel. Both types of vests were only capable of stopping low-velocity projectiles, however, and did little in the way of stopping high-powered rifle bullets.

The big "breakthrough" in the development of modern ballistic armor was the creation of the aramid fibers called Kevlar ("Kevlar" is a registered trade name used by Du Pont for the aramid fiber). Kevlar was created in the 1960s and became commercially available in 1972. Demand for the fiber quickly grew so that a decade later, Du Pont was selling over 45 million pounds of the material annually.

The aramid fiber was originally marketed for use in strengthening radial tire belts but soon found applications in protective clothing, cables, and protective housing equipment. Its resistance to heat also made it ideal in areas where asbestos-type material was needed.

Du Pont currently manufactures two types of Kevlar: Kevlar 29 and Kevlar 49. The former is generally used in ballistic vests, and Kevlar 49—even though it is a bit stronger—is most often used for plastic reinforcement of parts. (This is because Kevlar 49 is less rigid than Kevlar 29 so that it allows more energy to be transferred through it in a vest, which results in greater wounds behind the fabric if hit.) Occasionally, both are combined in different ratios to tailor the fibers to a specific use.

Kevlar 29 is five times as strong as steel, ten times as strong as aluminum, and has a density about half that of fiberglass. It doesn't melt and can be used without degradation at temperatures ranging from −320°F to 360°F; it doesn't burn and only starts to carbonize at 800°F.

Because Kevlar is a flexible fiber, it can be woven into cloth. Such cloth is strong enough to stop high-speed projectiles and—in layers—bullets. (Interestingly, the Kevlar cloth does not always stop sharp weapons like ice picks or very sharp knives because the points of the objects can "work" their way through the fabric. However, such weapons are considerably less effective against a person wearing a vest than they would be when attacking an unprotected person. Apparently, vests are about 98 percent effective in stopping knife attacks.)

Following the wave of social unrest, assassinations, and the increase in police shooting deaths in the 1960s, the Justice Department asked the U.S. Army to start working on bullet-resistant vests which might be used by civilians. This work was handled by the Department of Defense's BTEC (Ballistic Test and Evaluation Center) at Edgewood, MD. BTEC had been testing Kevlar for use with military vests, so the material was used in the first crude vests created for the Justice Department.

By 1973 BTEC had a number of articles of bullet-resistant clothing, including a sportcoat and raincoat with zip-out Kevlar linings. While these were crude by current standards, they did show the possibilities offered by Kevlar, and the Justice Department funded a research and development project which created five thousand one-and-a-half pound vests which were tested by fifteen police departments across the U.S. This trial run proved that vests were practical in protecting policemen.

In the early 1970s, the PPAA (Personal Protective Armor Association) was formed to create industry standards for manufacturers. Though the PPAA had the support of the U.S. Law Enforcement Association and the IACP (International Association of Chiefs of Police), it did not operate smoothly, and accomplished very little in setting up standards for the industry.

In the mid-seventies, work was started toward finding out more about how Kevlar fibers worked and how they might be incorporated into vests by the U.S. Army, the Law Enforcement Assistant Administration, and the National Bureau of Standards. One document of interest produced during this period is Body Armor For Law Enforcement Officers #027-000-00409-1, printed in 1976 by the U.S. Government. The 113-page report gives much technical information about Kevlar.

Among the discoveries was that the depth to which a bullet will penetrate layers of Kevlar varies in relation to the bullet's speed, material, and caliber (cross-sectional size). In general, the larger the diameter and slower the speed, the less the bullet's penetration. Lead bullets, which deform quickly, shed their speed more quickly in Kevlar than those made of steel or brass.

The angle at which a bullet hits the fabric is also important. Kevlar fabric slows down a bullet most efficiently when the bullet strikes the fabric perpendicularly. When the bullet strikes at an acute angle or near the edge of the fabric, it will penetrate more layers because less of the surface area of the fabric will be absorbing the energy of the bullet. This degradation is not too great but can be a consideration; most manufacturers of body armor add several layers of Kevlar fabric to vests to provide protection from shots arriving from an angle or which impact near the edge of a vest.

The type of weave and size of thread used in Kevlar fabric also have varying effects on the various types of projectiles the fabric will stop. In general, however, these differences are very small and seem to be more of a sales gimmick among manufacturers rather than an important consideration in how Kevlar fabric will perform. (The theory is that the best protection against small-caliber bullets is offered by small threads, while larger threads work best with the bigger bullets. Thus, some manufacturers make vests with layers of different-sized fibers and weaves in them to stop a wide variety of bullet sizes.)

Research also found that armor made of one piece of fabric was considerably stronger than armor made of multiple, separate layers of Kevlar. This was especially true as the edge of the vest was approached. Cut material tended to be weak at the edge, while folded Kevlar proved to be strong. (This is why many companies used a folded pad of cloth for an insert on carriers or to increase the stopping power of the vest by inserting the pad. The new U.S. Army helmets made of Kevlar are also created from one piece of folded fabric to create maximum strength with a minimum amount of material.)

Multiple hits of bullets or other high-speed projectiles in the exact same spot on Kevlar will degrade the material's protective properties, but the chances of this are very small—even with an automatic weapon fired point-blank. In tests conducted with both the firearm and vest stationary, it takes a number of such projectiles hitting in exactly the same spot to defeat a vest.

Thus, the chances of a vest which is adequate for a single hit being defeated by multiple hits on the same location is very small since both the shooter and the wearer of the vest will be moving.

Because Kevlar cloth bends and allows freedom of movement as well as protection, it is generally known as "soft armor" by those who work with ballistic armor designs. Soft armor is not without problems. For one thing, even though a projectile may be completely stopped by the Kevlar, some of the energy is transferred through the fabric onto the wearer's skin. This creates a wound similar to that created when one is struck with a very blunt object. This type of injury is called "blunt trauma" by those in the ballistic-armor industry.

Much controversy was created by early ballistic vests which were able to stop bullets but the blunt trauma created by the force of the bullets allowed the deaths of test animals. Since then, however, soft armor design has greatly improved: it appears that blunt trauma is not as great a consideration as it once was, except perhaps when large-caliber bullets hit directly over the heart or such hard bones as the skull. (Interestingly, a ballistic vest hit by a bullet which exceeds the vest's protective rating will often stop the bullet, but the blunt trauma is great enough to disable the wearer. Penetration is thus often less of a concern than the trauma, especially with vests which have few layers of Kevlar.)

In 1977, the U.S. NILECJ (National Institute of Law Enforcement and Criminal Justice) working in conjunction with the Aerospace Corporation created the "Body Armor Program Executive Summary," which has become the standard for testing vests in the United States.

Because of the debacle created by the excessive blunt trauma produced by early vests, the NILECJ test guidelines suggested the use of Roma Plastalina #1 modeling clay, within specific temperature ranges, to gauge the amount of energy transmitted through the vest material. Thus, a bullet must not only be stopped by a vest, but the deformation of the clay behind the vest

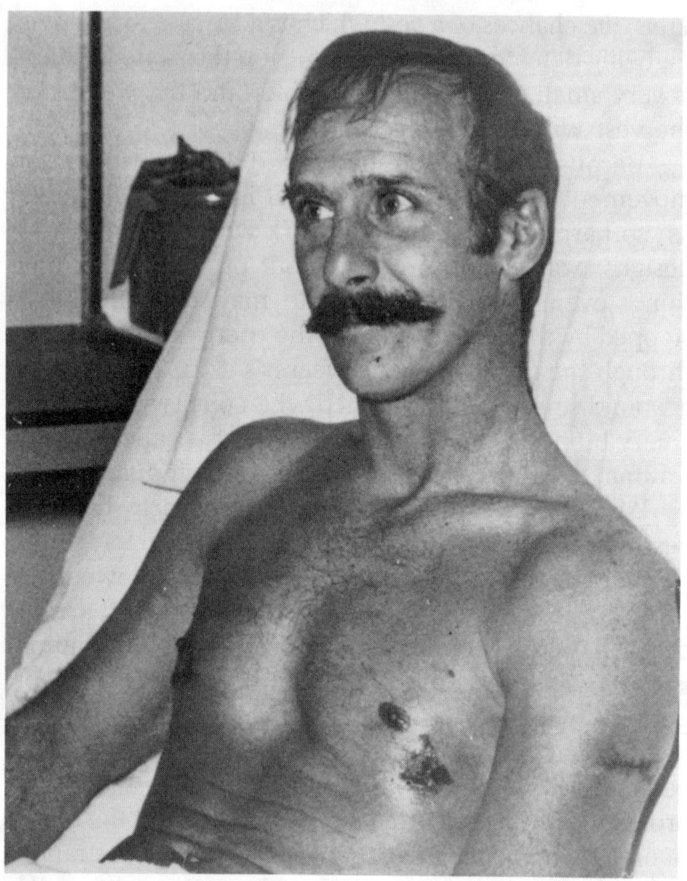

Blunt trauma created by bullets is not too great a problem provided the protection level of the vest is adequate. Officer Steve Gazdik was shot twice in the chest with a .357 Magnum fired from one inch and four inches; his Second Chance vest stopped both bullets. A third shot grazed his left arm. Photo courtesy of Second Chance Body Armor, Inc.

must be less than 1.73 inches.

There is much controversy as to how serious the blunt trauma produced when a vest stops a high-energy projectile is to the human body. While most authorities agree that such shock, if within the standards set by the NILECJ guidelines, is not serious when it occurs over soft tissue, there is uncertainty about hits on areas with hard bones close to the surface of the skin. One school maintains that buyers need not be overly concerned with the effects of blunt trauma other than to realize that they'll often have a whopper of a bruise when a bullet is stopped by their vest. The other school maintains that wearers may suffer grave injuries if a projectile hits areas over the sternum, ribs, or backbone. Consequently, some companies offer shockpads or extra armor over the heart, back and the kidneys, while others do not. Both sides have actual shooting cases to support their conflicting views, which causes no end to the confusion.

Another problem which soft armor may exhibit is a puckering or bunching up of the material when it is hit. This appears to be caused by the vacuum created behind a bullet, which pulls air into the vest and causes it to stretch and expand. A second hit in such an area will be apt to defeat more layers of Kevlar in such a situation because the various layers of Kevlar won't be supporting each other. Again, however, this is not as serious a problem as it might appear since most modern vests have stitching to prevent this puckering of the material and are worn with straps to prevent such movement. A few companies use "trauma pads" or extra stitching to prevent a puckering effect, but the trade-off is a very stiff vest which offers little more protection.

Kevlar's major disadvantage is that it can deteriorate over time. This deterioration is especially evident in the presence of ultraviolet light. Because of this tendency, modern vests are covered with ultraviolet-screening fabric, or the Kevlar itself is coated with a dye which has the same effect. Whatever protective measure is taken, if soft armor is to be used outdoors, it is important that the fabric is shielded from ultraviolet light (which is present in sunlight and can penetrate clouds, and which is also emitted from artificial bulbs).

Just how far this deterioration can go was shown during a recent test of police vests which had been in service for six years. Du Pont discovered that several of the used vests completely failed to stop 9mm bullets which they were designed to stop, while other vests showed an 11- to 24-percent reduction in their protective abilities. Du Pont found that much of the failure was actually in the form of "back face signature," the amount of fabric deformation into the wearer's body, which would probably have translated into excessive blunt shock trauma. The company believes that the majority of the vests tested had been degraded by exposure to ultraviolet light.

Deterioration also results when a vest is exposed to either alkalies or mineral acids. Unfortunately, human sweat and the various types of fungi and bacteria that grow in the sweaty, humid conditions found in vests worn for extended periods create the chemicals which will break down Kevlar fibers. Thus, vests can become quite unreliable after five years of heavy use without periodic and careful cleaning. Bleaches or cleaning agents containing bleaches are strong alkalies and should *not* be used to clean Kevlar since they create more damage to the fabric than no cleaning at all.

At the time of this writing, it appears that there *may* be some degradation of the protective ability of Kevlar coated with polyvinyl acetate, which is sometimes used to waterproof vests.

When Kevlar soft armor is wet, its ability to stop high-speed projectiles is temporarily decreased while it remains wet (water does *not* damage Kevlar). When the fabric is saturated with water, the stopping power is downgraded by 40 percent. Such conditions are rare, however. Under normal "rain-soaked" conditions or when the wearer is sweating, the fabric's protective factor is diminished only slightly. (Thus, though waterproofing the fabric sounds like a necessity, it actually isn't unless the vest is worn by personnel who might be in water for ten minutes or more during normal activities.)

Most modern military "flak" jackets are now made with layers of Kevlar inside them rather than ballistic nylon or ceramic/fiberglass inserts (which had a tendency to shatter and create large wounds when they were defeated). Kevlar is about the only material currently being used in soft armor.

However, to achieve the highest levels of protection with soft armor, steel inserts are often used (some manufacturers will look at this as "hard armor" or "hardening"). Although slightly heavier than ceramic plates, steel plates are cheaper to manufacture and are more resistant to breakage. When steel plates are backed by standard-style soft armor, their capability is augmented to the point that even the .308

To achieve the highest levels of protection with modern armor, steel inserts are often used. When steel plates are backed by standard-style soft armor, their capability is augmented to the point where even the .308 Winchester/7.62mm NATO armor-piercing bullet can be stopped by the armor. Shown is the "Hardcorps 4" vest. Photo courtesy of Second Chance Body Armor, Inc.

Winchester/7.62mm NATO armor-piercing bullet can be stopped by the armor. Most ballistic vests using steel plates are constructed like standard soft vests with pockets in which to carry the steel plates. This also gives the wearer the option of greatly lightening the vest when the dangers of being shot are smaller.

By using the fiber in conjunction with resins like those used to make fiberglass, it's also possible to mold Kevlar into "composite" materials or armor. These composites find use in new ballistic helmets and lightweight vehicle armor, and are even used to create nuclear blast-resistant command posts for use by the military. When used in ballistic armor in this manner, even though the Kevlar is still the major component which gives strength to the material, it is generally classed as "composite armor" rather than soft armor to show that it has a different quality from the flexible woven material.

Composite armor can be created with other materials as well. Fiberglass, graphite fibers, and metal fibers can all be used with resin to form tough sheets which—with the proper thickness—will stop bullets and shrapnel.

While fiberglass composite armor has to be thicker than Kevlar armor to stop equivalent ballistic projectiles, it is also cheaper to make and purchase. Therefore, fiberglass composite armor is often used where cost is more of a consideration than weight. Vehicles, speakers' podiums, bank counters, guard stations, etc., all are ideal areas where fiberglass composite armor can be utilized to save money without a reduction in protection.

Lucite, Plexiglas G, and polycarbonate plastics can all be used to create clear, bullet-resistant windows and doors. When such plastics are used, they create much stronger barriers than does glass. When used outside or for protective masks, these materials should be coated with clear abrasive-resistant and ultraviolet-blocking plastics.

Currently, several companies are using these materials to create "custom" ballistic armor for businesses and politicians. Such custom work can be done to automobiles or to many types of buildings, including both business structures and homes. Among the companies doing this type of work or offering materials to local contractors for such customizing are Point Blank, Composite Technologies, and Almac Plastics, Inc.

COMPARATIVE PROPERTIES OF MODERN BALLISTIC MATERIALS

Fiber	Tensile Strength (lb/in²)	Elongation (%)	Density (lb/in²)
Kelvar 29	400,000	3.6	0.052
Reinforced Kevlar 29 (resin)	525,000	4.4	0.052
Kevlar 49	400,000	2.5	0.052
Reinforced Kevlar 49 (resin)	525,000	2.9	0.052
Nylon	143,000	18.3	0.041
Dacron (Type 68)	162,500	14.5	0.050
Stainless Steel	250,000	2.0	0.283
High-Strength Graphite	450,000	1.25	0.063
"E" Glass	350,000	3.5	0.092
Asbestos	100,000	1.7	0.090

In 1984, companies involved in manufacturing and marketing ballistic vests decided to reactivate the PPAA in an effort to stop some of the squabbling among the various companies and to create a standard for labeling and testing vests, as well as guidelines for selling vests to civilian users. The PPAA ended up with thirty members, including many armor manufacturers, dealers, distributors, weaving mills, and even Du Pont.

2: Ballistic Vests

The most common body armor is the "bulletproof vest."

Modern bullet-resistant vests made of Kevlar work well. Although they offer limited protection, they do protect the major body organs (except the brain) and greatly improve the wearer's chances of survival when attacked. Currently, 37 percent of most shootings involve wounds to the head with three percent of the wounds occurring to the neck, three percent to the arms, and one percent to the legs; the rest are to the chest, stomach, sides, or back. This means that a shooting victim wearing a vest giving full-torso coverage will stand to receive about 56 percent fewer wounds than a counterpart not wearing a vest. While it is, of course, impossible to predict what type of wounds will occur in any given conflict, the wearer of a ballistic vest certainly enjoys a greater chance of surviving a gun fight.

In addition to stopping bullets, balistic vests will often give protection from other sharp objects, such as axes, knives, and broken glass bottles. Ballistic vests won't stop all pointed or bladed weapons since some pointed knives and ice picks can penetrate between the threads in the Kevlar weave *if* the point of the weapon hits the vest at a 90-degree angle. But wearing a vest is a lot better than not wearing one at all against such attacks. Vests often give full protection from edged weapons since it is hard to achieve a 90-degree attack, and most attackers don't realize that vests can be defeated from a thrust of that angle. Vests also offer some protection during auto accidents, and not a few vest wearers have walked away from what could normally have been a fatal accident because the vest stopped the penetration of glass and metal.

Currently, Vector is offering a "chain mail" undershirt/vest which will be capable of stopping more, if not all, knife or ice-pick attacks. Made of two-inch squares of tough plastic, the vest units lock up with outside pressure so that any hit is spread out over a wide area. Wearers of such a vest would also be able to take strikes to the torso with clubs without adverse effects. Such vests are aimed at the growing market of prison guards and those who may be confronting rioters. The vests do not offer ballistic protection by themselves but are easily coupled with ballistic vests to give double protection.

Ballistic vests made of Kevlar are currently rated according to how powerful a bullet they will stop. Since higher velocity bullets can only be stopped with more layers of Kevlar or steel inserts, the more a vest can stop, the more expensive it is. It will also be heavier, hotter to wear (since the greater thickness stops air flow), and less concealable. These drawbacks are important considerations for those who have to wear the vests for extended periods or who may face opponents who will try head shots if they suspect vests are being worn. Because of these factors, heavy vests are usually reserved for use by police SWAT units or in military combat, while lighter vests are used by dignitaries and policemen since the lighter vests offer protection from the weapons assailants normally use.

The NILECJ study of 1977 set up the guidelines for vest testing which are still currently used by vest manufacturers to rate their armor. These tests lead to

Heavy vests like this "Hardcorps 3" are usually reserved for use with police SWAT units or in military combat. The vest is capable of stopping shell fragments, shotgun and pistol projectiles. With ballistic panel inserts, its protection factor can be increased to Level III or IV. Photo courtesy of Second Chance Body Armor, Inc.

ratings for the vests which, in turn, allow the buyer of a vest to know, more or less, what the vest can stop in the way of bullets. The protection varies, however, since the type of bullet and barrel length of a weapon can make a big difference as to whether or not the vest will give protection. (It should also be remembered that a fly-by-night company might set up their own "tests" and sell vests which don't stop what the company claimed. Vests should only be purchased from reputable dealers.)

The protection levels are divided into four types with the second, "Type II," being divided up, for reasons making sense only to the original testers, into two divisions, Type II-A and Type II. Currently, some companies have also added "I+" and "II+" to the system to show that their vest will stop a bit more than the normal I- or II-rated vests.

In general, eight layers of Kevlar are needed for Level I protection and sixteen layers for Level II. But the amount of layers needed is not "hard and fast;" most companies vary the weave and types of Kevlar so that the number of layers used varies from one company to the next. Additionally, most add several layers to cover the possibility that shots may hit the vest from an angle or puffing up of vest material may occur.

The table below will give you some idea as to the types of bullets vests will stop according to their ratings.

PROTECTION OFFERED BY VESTS

Threat	Type I	Type II-A	Type II	Type III-A	Type IV
.22 LR (Handgun)	Yes	Yes	Yes	Yes	Yes
.25 Auto	Yes	Yes	Yes	Yes	Yes
.32 Auto	Yes	Yes	Yes	Yes	Yes
.380 Auto	Yes	Yes	Yes	Yes	Yes
.38 Special (lead)	Yes	Yes	Yes	Yes	Yes
.44 Special	Yes	Yes	Yes	Yes	Yes
12 Gauge (shot)	Yes	Yes	Yes	Yes	Yes
.22 LR (Rifle)	No	Yes	Yes	Yes	Yes
.25 Auto KTW	No	Yes	Yes	Yes	Yes
.380 Auto KTW	No	Yes	Yes	Yes	Yes
.38 Special	No	Yes	Yes	yes	Yes
.38 Special +P	No	Yes	Yes	Yes	Yes
.45 Auto	No	Yes	Yes	Yes	Yes
.45 Auto KTW	No	Yes	Yes	Yes	Yes
9mm Luger (JSP)	No	Yes	Yes	Yes	Yes
9mm Luger (SuperVel)	No	Yes	Yes	Yes	Yes
.38 Super	No	Yes	Yes	Yes	Yes
12 Gauge (Buckshot)	No	Yes	Yes	Yes	Yes
.357 Magnum (JSP)	No	No	Yes	Yes	Yes
.44 Magnum (lead)	No	No	Yes	Yes	Yes
.44 Magnum (JSP)	No	No	Yes	Yes	Yes
9mm Luger (FMJ)	No	No	No	Yes	Yes
.38 Special KTW	No	No	No	Yes	Yes
9mm Luger KTW	No	No	No	Yes	Yes
.357 Magnum KTW	No	No	No	Yes	Yes
.44 Magnum KTW	No	No	No	Yes	Yes
.30 Carbine	No	No	No	Yes	Yes
12 Gauge (Slug)	No	No	No	Yes	Yes
.308 Win. FMJ	No	No	No	Yes	Yes
.30-06 (Soft Point)	No	No	No	Yes	Yes
7.62mm Soviet (AP)	No	No	No	No	Yes
7.62mm NATO (AP)	No	No	No	No	Yes
5.56mm NATO (AP)	No	No	No	No	Yes
.30-06 (AP)	No	No	No	No	Yes

(Note: Because of new developments in both armor and ammunition, this chart is included herein to provide the reader with a general idea of a modern vest's capabilities. Be sure to check with the vest manufacturer for the precise type of projectiles a particular vest will actually protect against.)

Because of the "arms race" that is currently taking place in the criminal sector, Level I vests are nearly obsolete. While they offer better protection than no vest at all, most people needing a vest would be much safer wearing one that is rated at least II-A, with II being an even better choice.

Currently, armor-piercing bullets and the "cop killer" KTW bullets are not too great a concern to policemen or civilians worried about criminal attack. Neither type of ammunition is easy to find (or make) and isn't very effective as a fight-stopper except with high-velocity bullets. While these are common on battlefields, the chances of encountering such rounds in civilian areas is pretty small at the time of this writing.

Provided the news media don't make armor-piercing bullets or KTW rounds sound like *the* best thing to use in a gun, the bullets should remain fairly rare. Also, at the time of this writing, Congress is considering passing a bill to outlaw such rounds. Though criminals will undoubtedly still be able to make or purchase such ammunition if they so desire, the armor-piercing bullets should become a little harder to obtain. Their poor combat performance when hitting flesh and blood should make them rare except on the battlefield. (To date, there are no known cases of a policeman's ballistic vest being defeated by armor-piercing bullets. The number of policemen shot in the head has increased after media coverage of police use of ballistic armor, however, as more criminals realize that ballistic vests are being used. The simple expedient for the criminal is to make head shots rather than to locate the rare and expensive "cop killer" bullets. In reality, the KTW rounds were originally designed at the request of the law-enforcement community and the "cop killer" bullet is a myth created by the media.

Another legislative "solution" to crime that would make much of the body armor now on the market of little use would be a ban on handguns. A number of studies have suggested that a handgun ban would actually have an adverse effect on those owning ballistic vests since criminals would probably turn to sawed-off shotguns and rifles to use in crime. While shotguns are not much of a consideration with modern ballistic vests, most rifle bullets are since many of the rifle calibers penetrate all but the heaviest of vests. Just as the ban on the importation of cheap handguns into the United States caused larger calibers and better handguns to be used by criminals thereby making the Level I vest nearly obsolete, a ban on all types of handguns or similar legislation would probably create a situation in which criminals would use much more dangerous weapons than they now are using.

From time to time there are movements in many states as well as federal legislatures to ban the sale of vests to civilians so that criminals can't get vests to wear. Like other bans, this may sound appealing but probably wouldn't be too practical. It may turn out that the police and politicians would all have legal vests, the criminals would have boot-leg vests, and Joe Average would be out in the cold. At any rate, if you need a vest and aren't "connected" to a group that would still be able to own vests should restrictive legislation be enacted, it may be wise to purchase one now so that you may not have to be subjected to a lot of hassle and red tape.

Because Kevlar loses very little of its protective value when wet by sweat, waterproof coatings on Kevlar vests are not necessary and may even cut down on the protective life of the Kevlar. Furthermore, such coatings will actually make the vests hotter to wear. Therefore, when possible, try to avoid Kevlar products which have been treated by anything other than resins.

One way of decreasing the excessive retention of

body heat and moisture under a vest is to wear the special T-shirts most vest manufacturers offer with their vests. Another solution to the problem is to encase the vest in a cotton carrier; cotton tends to wick the moisture out of the vest and cools off the wearer somewhat in the process. Minimizing the regular clothing worn over the vest and removal of the side panels of the vests (when this is possible) will also help out during extremely hot weather. When vests become damp, it is also wise to fully air them out before wearing them (a hair drier can be used to dry the vest since heat doesn't damage Kevlar).

Manufacturers have done a good job of offering a wide variety of styles and sizes of ballistic vests for both men and women; many models are also adjustable through the use of Velcro connectors and straps which hold the vest tightly in place. While these adjustment straps can make one vest fit several people, each vest should be carefully chosen for the proper size, fit, maximum concealability, and comfort for the individual who is to wear it. Also, because of the high amount of maintenance needed to keep ballistic vests from deteriorating, it's better to have one person responsible for his own vest than to have several people care for it, as they may each expect the other to care for the vest.

Many companies sell ballistic vests. Probably the oldest and best known of these companies is Second Chance. This company has a very good reputation with the law-enforcement community and offers a wide selection of vests. The next most popular company is American Body Armor. It, too, offers a wide range of vests and has products which are chosen by many in the law-enforcement community. Other top-notch companies are Point Blank Body Armor and Silent Partner. Of these four companies, Point Blank has the widest variety of vests and ballistic products currently available from one source.

Unfortunately, these companies and lesser contenders in the armor business have, in their advertising,

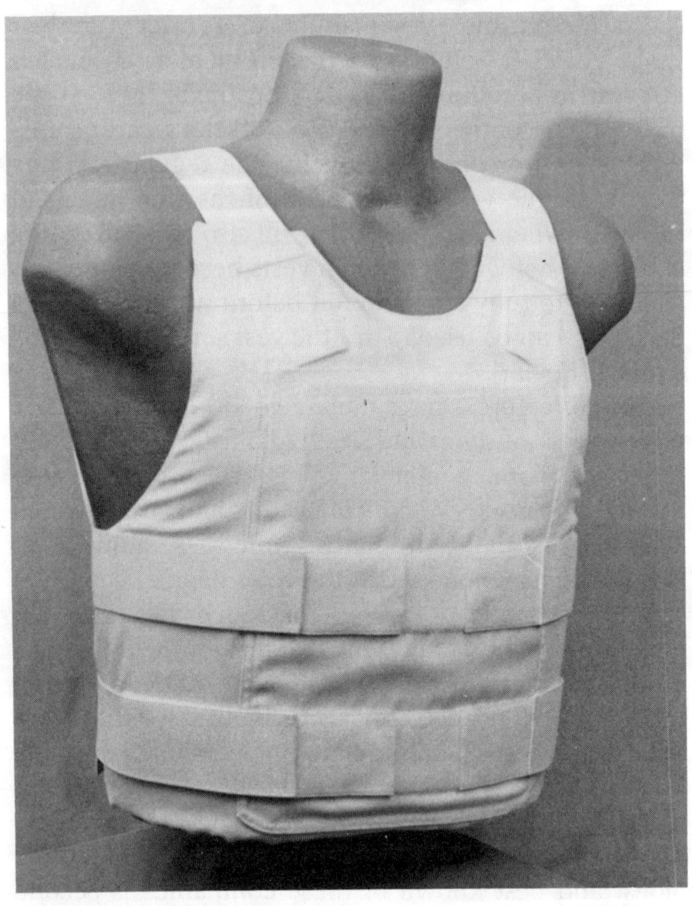

Manufacturers have done a good job of offering a wide variety of styles and sizes of ballistic vests both for men and women; many models of vests are also adjustable through the use of Velcro connectors and straps which hold the vest tightly in place. Photo courtesy of Second Chance Body Armor, Inc.

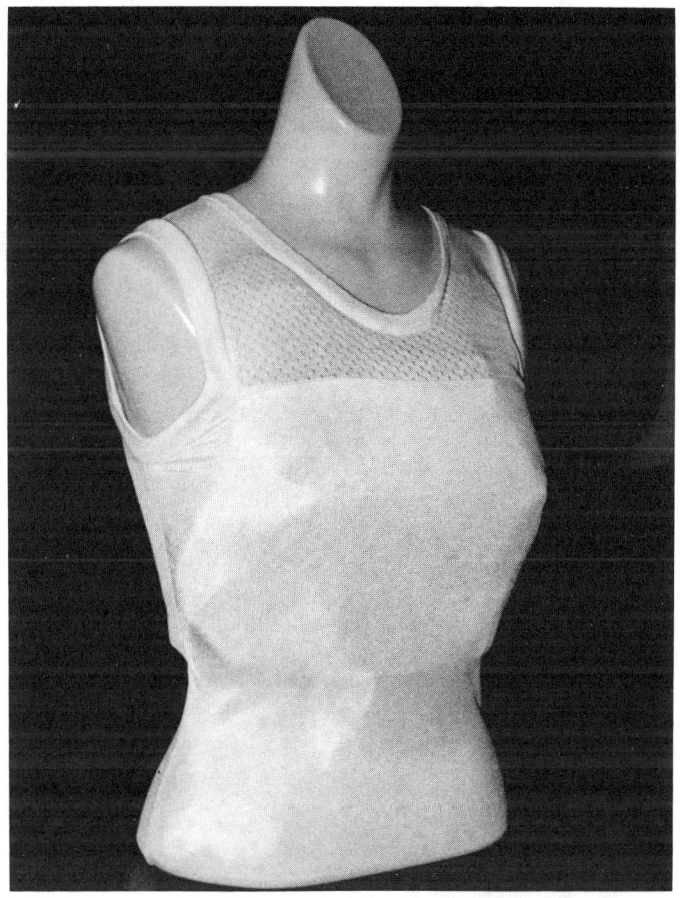

Lightweight and form-fitting, this vest gives a high level of protection without calling attention to itself. Photo courtesy of Second Chance Body Armor, Inc.

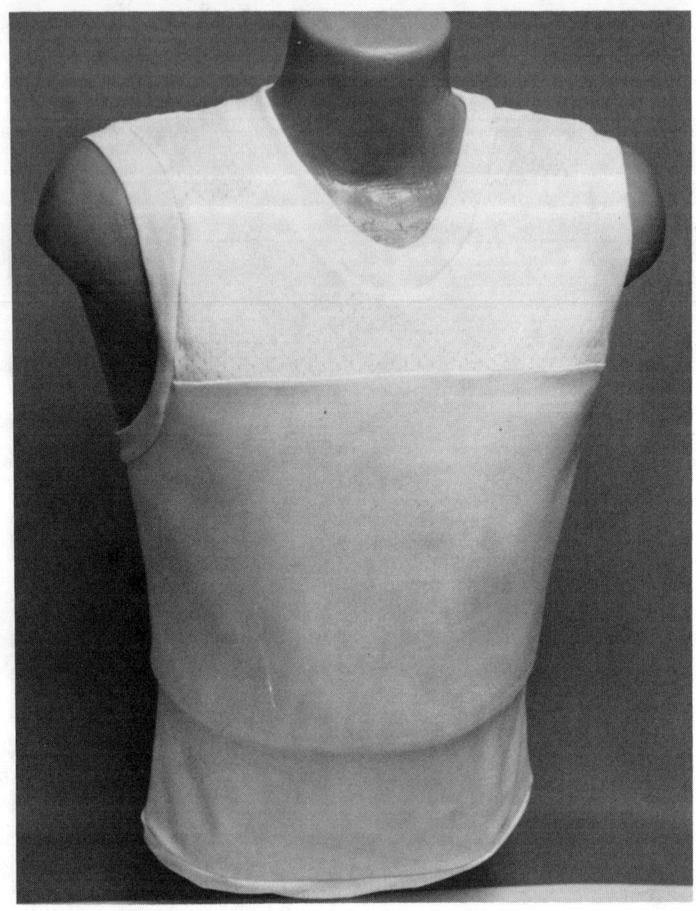

Designed for maximum concealment and comfort, this ballistic vest uses a T-shirt-style carrier to allow the user to wear it comfortably. Photo courtesy of Second Chance Body Armor, Inc.

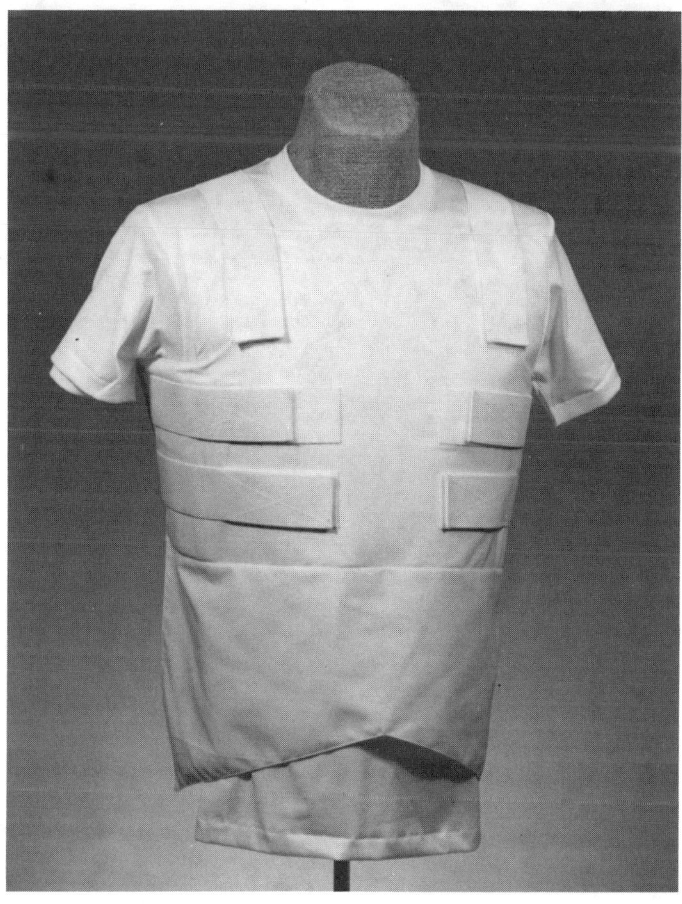

Silent Partner's "Traditional" vest, like those of many other manufacturers, uses adjustable straps with Velcro connectors which hold the vest tightly in place. Photo courtesy of Silent Partner.

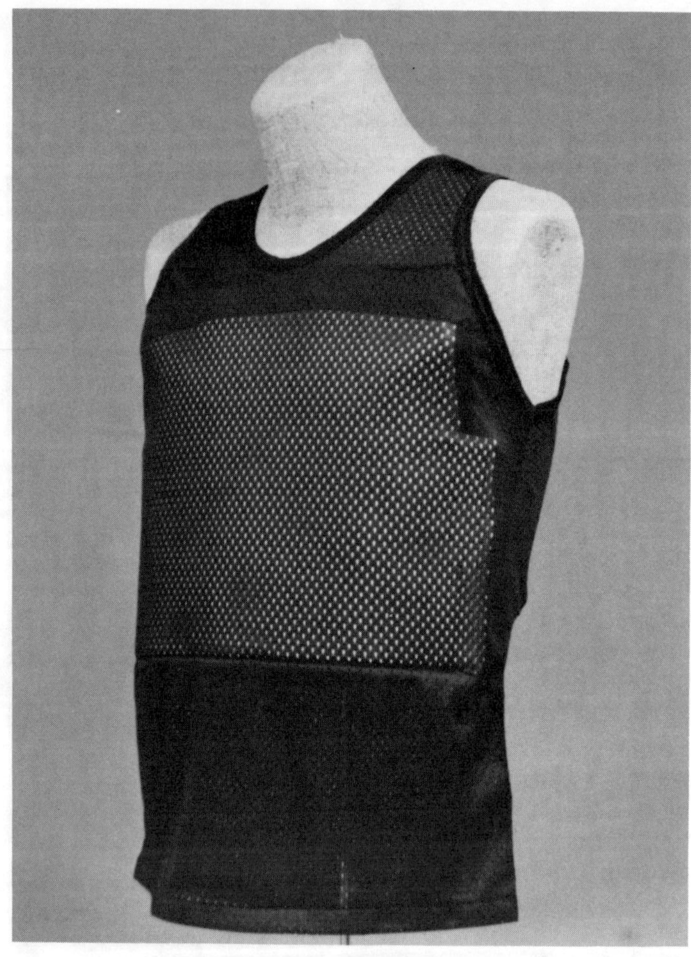

Silent Partner's "Super Shirt" minimizes heat buildup while the vest is worn through good design. This lightweight carrier allows Kevlar inserts to be added to create a modular system of variable protection. Another plus: the vest is very easy to conceal. Photo courtesy of Silent Partner.

resorted to name-calling and often emphasize the faults of their competitors' products while trying to sell their own. In fact, all offer very good products. Probably the best bet is to shop for a vest style and price that best suits the buyer; at the time of this writing all companies offer excellent vests. (Also important to keep in mind is the fact that Second Chance and American Body

Armor are not currently selling vests to civilians.)

When shopping for a vest, write or call all the manufacturers and ask for catalogues. After you've found several models which you wish to purchase, compare prices and make your decision. If you are part of an organization which needs a number of vests, it may be possible to get special quotes for prices or even have a company representative come out to fit your personnel.

If you need a large number of vests, a factory representative may offer to come out to your area and demonstrate the vests. While the demonstration can be very informative, don't be overly influenced by tests which show how a competitor's product fails while the company representative's product out-performs it. Unfortunately, hanky-panky has been known to take place during such performances.

Because of the rivalry among companies, Second Chance has gone so far as to print a list of things to watch for when a comparison test is being made between vests by a factory representative. Their recommendations are as follows:

1. When a shot is fired at a vest and the vest "puffs up," insist that the vest be patted down before another shot is fired at it. When the vest is puffed up, it can be defeated more easily. Such puffing doesn't normally occur in vests which are worn under clothing, strapped in place, or in a cloth carrier; puffing up isn't much of a consideration except on vests designed to be worn over clothing.

2. Use a magnet to check the bullets being fired at the vest. According to Second Chance, sales representatives sometimes use armor-piercing bullets against their competitor's vests. The same type of ammunition should be used on both vests.

3. When vests are tested, they should be obtained directly from the companies involved, not supplied by the company representative. Even assuming that the vests are actually the standard vests from the various companies, there's no way to prove that they came

directly from the company, and the test will prove little.

4. Be sure comparable levels of protection are taken into consideration when comparing vests and costs. (Don't let manufacturers model numbers confuse you; some "Model 2's" may give only II-A protection, etc.)

5. Remember that the test should show the protection given to the wearer of the vest. Occasionally tests are carried out which, purposely or inadvertently, compare vests on a basis of whether a round will go clear through them. What should be tested is whether a vest will keep a bullet from going halfway through it into the area the owner of the vest will occupy.

6. Finally, watch out for the tricks that are as old as the art of salesmanship. Being told that so-and-so company is about to go (or has gone) out of business or that someone was killed while demonstrating X company's vest, are examples of salesmanship which should arouse a little skepticism on the part of the listener.

In addition to standard, concealable vests, most companies also offer military/SWAT-style vests, "quilted" vests which accept ballistic panels, and vests which appear to be dress vests worn with suits but which are actually "classy" ballistic vests. These dress vests are available in a wide variety of colors and usually appear to button down the front like standard vests even though they, in fact, button up on the side. This allows a full ballistic panel to go across the front of the vest. Several companies also offer raincoats in a variety of colors and styles with ballistic vests built into them; probably the most successful of these is Point Blanks' "Ballistic Raincoat" which offers protection from Class I to III-A.

By purchasing the ballistic panels from various companies and engaging the services of a good tailor or seamstress, it is also possible to customize your own clothing to create ballistic jackets, vests, or what-have-you. If possible, the panels should be fastened into clothing in such a manner that the panels won't droop

This nylon jacket is available in a variety of colors and appears ordinary. It contains ballistic panels which make it into a very practical ballistic vest. Photo courtesy of Second Chance Body Armor, Inc.

and so that they can easily be removed and placed in other clothing.

In addition to commercial vests, military-surplus "flak jackets" are available on the market which offer various levels of protection. Current federal law requires that such vests be "demilitarized," meaning that a slash has to be made through the Kevlar material as well as the fabric carrier. However, it's often possible to repair such vests by combining several of these vests to create a whole one; this is often done either by the military-surplus outlet or the buyer interested in a do-it-yourself-type kit.

Such surplus vests certainly offer a monetary savings in many cases, but the buyer has no idea of whether or not the Kevlar in the vest has deteriorated, how adequately it has been mended (unless it is a do-it-yourself job), or what protection level the vest gives. These vests are designed to be worn over clothing so that the vest is in no way concealable except perhaps under a heavy winter coat. Therefore, surplus flak jackets are not too good a buy in most cases except for those fighting battles on a tight budget.

However, for the do-it-yourselfer, the Kevlar material inside the vests can be removed from the vests and tested. If the Kevlar appears to be in good shape, it could then be formed into a vest with a little time, patience, and the use of a heavy-duty sewing machine.

It's also possible to purchase new Kevlar from the companies listed in the appendix. While the Kevlar is more expensive than the surplus material, it will also be brand new and offer a maximum of performance.

Here are some of the commercial vests currently offered by the top four manufacturers. Remember that styles and protection levels of vests are constantly being changed. For up-to-date information, contact the companies directly (addresses are listed in the appendix of this book).

Opposite page, lower left: Without the ballistic panel inserts, this "Hardcorps 2" vest is an ideal flak jacket. With the inserts, it can stop nearly all conventional small-arms fire hitting it perpendicularly. Lower right: The "Command Jac" provides Level IV protection with the proper inserts. Photos courtesy of Second Chance Body Armor, Inc.

SECOND CHANCE VESTS

Model	Protection Level(s)	Approx. Weight (lbs)	Coverage
Checkmate	I+	2.3	Front/back
Deep Cover II	II, II-A	2.6-3.3	Front only
Standard SPA 17	II-A, II, III	5.2-6	Front/back
Mini-Rap SPA 17	II-A, II, III	5.5-6.2	Full
Maximum Concealable SPA 22	II-A, II, III	5.9-6.7	Full
Female Vest	IIA, II	3	Full
Command Jac	III (with K30 insert) IV (with K47 insert)		Full; maximum in front
Hardcorps 2	II (without inserts)	4	Front/back
	III (with K30 inserts)	8	Front; maximum
	IV (with K47 front inserts)	14.9	Front; maximum
Hardcorps 3	II (without inserts)	6.25	Full
	IV (with K47 front inserts)	18.6	Front; maximum
	IV front/III sides (with K47 and K30 inserts)	21	Front; maximum
Hardcorps 4	II	8	Full
	II (with K47 inserts)	19	Front; maximum

Note: Command Jac and Hardcorps vests are worn over other clothing and are non-concealable.

AMERICAN BODY ARMOR VESTS

Model	Protection Level(s)	Weight (lbs)	Coverage
K-10	I	1.7	Front/back
K10 MC	I	2.4	Full
K-27 MC	II-A (front), II (back)	3.2	Full
K-27 HD	II-A (front and back)	3.8	Full
K-15	II-A (front and back)	3.0	Front/back
K-15 HD	II	3.8	Front/back
K-27 MC Special	II	4.9	Full

Note: American Body Armor "Shok Plate" ballistic inserts will increase the level of protection in the front of the vest by roughly one step up the rating scale. Model specifications are subject to change. Most models have "shirt tails" optional to help keep the vest in place.

POINT BLANK VESTS

Model	Protection Level(s)	Weight (lbs)	Coverage
Close Encounter	I through II+	2 to 3.8	Front only
Close Encounter-SP	I through II+	2.6 to 4.5	Front only
Close Encounter (Female model)	I through II	2 to 3.5	Front only
ST-10	I	2	Front/back
CT-10	I	2.2	Front/back
SP-10	I	2.6	Full
FM-10 (Female)	I	2	Full
ST-15	II-A	3	Front/back
CT-15	II-A	3.2	Front/back
SP-15	II-A	3.5	Full
FM-15 (Female)	II-A	3	Full
ST-20	II	3.5	Front/back
CT-20	II	3.8	Front/back
SP-20	II	4.2	Full
FM-20	II	3.6	Full
ST-26	II or more	3.8	Front/back
CT-26	II or more	4.2	Front/back
SP-26	II or more	4.5	Full
ST-30	III-A	5.2	Front/back
CT-30	III-A	5.6	Front/back
SP-30	III-A	6.4	Full
Minute Man Series (100 SR, 150 SR, 200 SR, 260 SR, 300 SR)	I through III-A	2.6 to 6.4	Front/back or full
EV-15 (Entry Vest)	II-A	7.8	Front only
EV-20 (Entry Vest)	II	10.5	Front only

Model	Protection Level(s)	Weight (lbs)	Coverage
RV-10 (Recon Vest)	I	7	Full
RV-15 (Recon Vest)	II-A	9.5	Full
RV-20 (Recon Vest)	II	11.5	Full
RV-26 (Recon Vest)	II+	12	Full
RV-30 (Recon Vest)	III-A	15	Full
TAC-JAC 26	II+ (Plate increases protection to III or IV)	8.8 (16.3 with plate)	Full
TAC-JAC 30	III-A (Plate increases protection to III or IV)	11.8 (19.3 with plate)	Full
TACTICAL/ASSAULT	Identical to TAC-JAC but with groin protection and collar	7.5-10	Full plus groin
NATO/SWAT	Identical to TAC-JAC but with groin protection	5.5-7.6	Full plus groin
U.S FRAGMENTATION VEST	(Military Specifications only)	9	Full
Military Field Jacket Liner	I through III-A	6 to 12.8	Full
Prison Riot Vest	I	12	Full plus groin

SILENT PARTNER VESTS

Model	Protection Level(s)	Coverage
T-Shirt Carrier	I, II-A, or II	Front and/ or back
Tropical Carrier	I, II-A, or II	Front and/ or back
Super Shirt	I, II-A, or II	Front and/ or back
Lady SP (Female)	I, II-A, or II	Front and/ or back
Traditional	I, II-A, or II	Front/back or full
BETA (Building Entry Team Armor)	I to IV with inserts and ceramic plate	Front/back or full

Note: Silent Partner vests are more or less modular with the level of protection afforded by the vest being determined by the type of panel placed in it by the wearer. Protection can be only in the front, front and sides, or front, back, and sides depending on the panel combination. A panel of ceramic plates is used to increase the front panel of the BETA vest to Level IV.

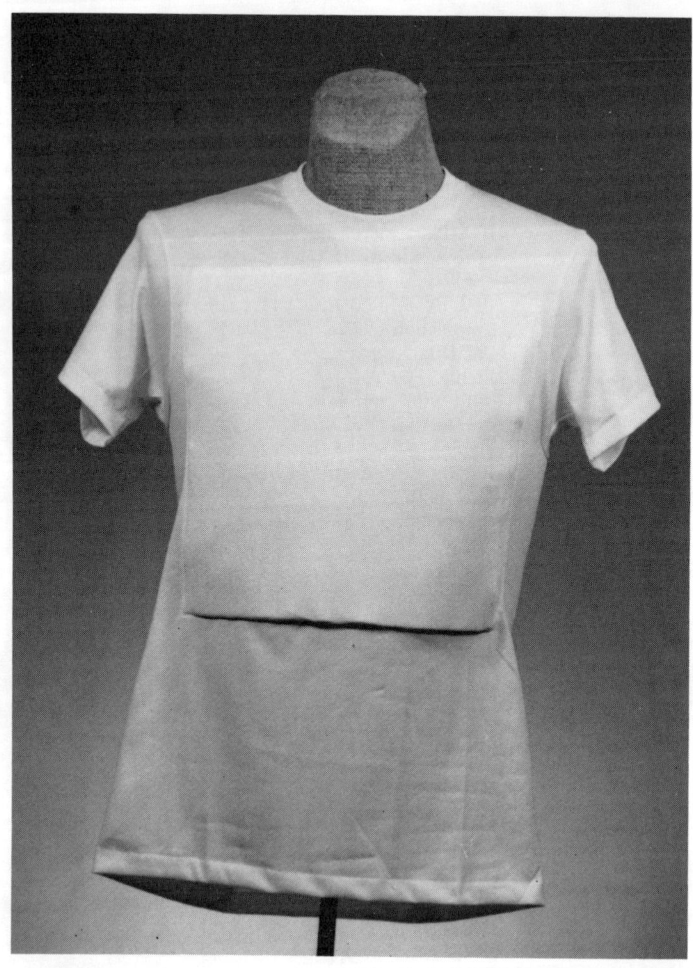

Silent Partner's "T-shirt" carrier allows the wearer to create the level of protection he needs through the use of Kevlar inserts to the front and, if he wishes, to the back. Long tails keep the vest from riding up the back. Photo courtesy of Silent Partner.

Because many people, especially police officers, are shot with their own weapons, it is wise to use only bullets that will *not* defeat your armor if you normally carry a firearm when wearing a vest (the only exception to this would be on the modern battlefield where usually enemies don't get close enough to "snatch" a weapon).

The best vest is the one you're wearing when under fire. A lightweight vest that is worn is better than a heavier one which remains in the closet. A lightweight vest may also be concealed more easily; an assailant who knows of your vest is likely to shoot at your head. This is Silent Partner's "Tropical Carrier." Photo courtesy of Silent Partner.

Like a lot of other tools, the best vest is the one you wear because it's comfortable and the one you have on when you need it. A lightweight vest that is worn is better than a heavy one that remains in a closet or locker. A little protection is better than none at all.

Remember, too, that a vest doesn't turn you into a Superman. Don't allow people to know that you're wearing a vest; otherwise, your next assailant may make a head shot.

3:

Ballistic Armor

There are a number of other pieces of armor other than the ballistic vest. Many of these are equally effective at reducing a wearer's injuries and—when coupled with a vest—can offer a lot of protection to the wearer.

Some of these items of ballistic armor are readily available in the marketplace while others are harder to find because there is such little demand for them that few companies make them. Others, like Kevlar gloves and polycarbonate goggles, are designed for use in areas other than personal protection and are found in unexpected areas like sporting goods stores or industrial suppliers.

HELMETS

Currently, 37 percent of most shootings involve wounds to the head. This means that the use of a good helmet capable of stopping the more common bullets would greatly improve a fighter's chances of survival.

There are several catches, however. One is that there are limits as to how much weight can be easily carried on the head. Also, some thought has to be given as to how the helmet might cut down on visibility and speaking ability. Finally, the helmet shouldn't be easy for an opponent to get a firm hold of (not a few soldiers have been killed because an enemy twisted them off their feet by grabbing a tightly fastened helmet).

More of a problem with helmet design from a ballistics standpoint is that because the skull lies so close to the surface of the skin, the head is unable to withstand the blunt trauma which often develops behind a bullet stopped by ballistic material. In the abdomen, such blunt trauma energy usually only causes a large bruise; on the scalp it can cause a concussion. Even if blunt trauma on the skull is avoided, the force of the impact can be transformed to a jolt or a whiplash, possibly resulting in damage to the brain when it "bounces" within the skull as the skull jerks violently.

Vector, one of the companies currently making ballistic helmets, has recorded readings of up to 400 Gs (400 times greater than the normal force of gravity) on ballistic helmets when each stopped a 9mm Luger bullet. While the helmets were successful in stopping a bullet, the good health of anyone wearing one after receiving such a jolt of energy would be in jeopardy. Researchers at Vector believe that human beings can withstand forces only up to the 100 to 200 G range without becoming "punchy." Therefore, the company makes all its helmets so that they'll keep the G forces under this level within the helmet's rated stopping power. (To get some idea of just how much potential force has to be dealt with, a 9mm Luger creates about 390 foot pounds of energy at its muzzle. Imagine a 390-pound gorilla dropping onto your head from one foot and you have an idea of what 390 foot-pounds would be like.)

Steel helmets offer almost no protection from bullets. Such helmets deflect low-velocity shrapnel, bullet/rock fragments, etc; they are better than nothing, but don't offer as much protection as we are sometimes led to believe.

The U.S. World War I vintage "Doughboy" helmet is a good example of poor design. The flat shape and wide brim were apparently created with an eye toward fashion. The helmet could be worn at a jaunty angle but offered little protection from anything but overhead, low-velocity shrapnel and had a tendency to be twisted askew when the wearer "hit the dirt." The helmet also gave an excellent grip to an enemy who grabbed the helmet from behind, and its width gave an enemy enough leverage to quickly break the wearer's neck if the chin strap were tightly fastened. In addition to these problems, the helmet apparently had a tendency to cause low-velocity projectiles to ricochet back into the wearer's scalp when they hit the helmet's inside rim.

Despite the many drawbacks, the Doughboy-style helmet remained the principal helmet for the British soldier through World War II (except for a jump helmet modeled after that used by German paratroopers). In the U.S., the Doughboy helmet was replaced just before World War II after over twenty years of service.

The U.S. soldier faired better during World War II with his "steel pot" helmet, as it offered more protection to the wearer's head and suffered from fewer problems than the Doughboy helmet. The steel helmet had a good suspension assembly and a helmet liner, both of which minimized blows received in hand-to-hand combat—no small consideration to those in the Pacific theater.

The "steel pot" continued to be issued to all troops up until the 1980s when Kevlar composite helmets started to be phased into U.S. military units. These new helmets are often referred to as "Fritz" helmets because they appear to be very similar to the Stahlhelm ("Steel Helmet") used by the Germans in World Wars I and II. In fact, the new helmets go a bit beyond the Stahlhelm in good design and have a more pronounced ridge around the front brim of the helmet and around the ears and neck than was present in the German helmets.

In composition, the new U.S. helmets are also quite different from the German namesake's. Made of Kevlar composite, the helmets are easily molded into shape and weigh only 3.2 pounds. Best of all, the helmets are capable of stopping most battlefield pistol/submachine rounds and many long-range rifle bullets or shell fragments traveling below 2,000 feet per second. The composite material also is less apt to show up in infrared detection scopes and can have a non-reflective finish according to the purchaser's needs. (Available finishes from Point Blank, for example, include Woodland Camouflage, Desert Camouflage, Snow Camouflage, and Olive Green.)

The U.S. military helmet is still designed principally for the deflection of shrapnel and is not normally rated for its ballistic level because of the high-G injury which might accompany it when it stopped a bullet. With most soldiers on the battlefield carrying rifles, the helmet will not stop most rounds which might be fired at it except from the unlikely ranges of over three hundred yards.

The U.S. Kevlar helmet was not the first composite helmet to be used by a military force. In fact, the Israeli ballistic helmet was issued a number of years prior to the U.S. helmets. The Israeli helmets closely resemble the World War II-vintage German jump helmet but have a much better strap and suspension system. Unlike the U.S. helmet which uses Kevlar for its ballistic protection, the Israeli helmet blends fiberglass, ballistic nylon, and Kevlar to give a Level II-A protection factor (which is roughly comparable to the protection factor of the U.S. helmet).

Because the Israeli helmet looks more like a policeman's motorcycle helmet, it is also easily adapted to use by SWAT teams or similar units. Therefore, it is currenlty offered in the U.S. through military surplus outlets, the most notable being Sherwood International. The three-pound helmet comes in medium and large sizes, and the olive green finish is easily painted to go with a variety of uniforms. Current cost is slightly less than $100.

A group of ballistic helmets created specifically for stopping pistol bullets (rather than shrapnel) has been developed for law-enforcement use by Vector. These helmets have a less "militaristic" look to them and are designed in the general shape of the policeman's motorcycle helmet for the most part.

This ballistic helmet has been developed for law-enforcement use. It is designed in the general shape of the policeman's motorcycle helmet and gives maximum head protection from many of the dangers facing the "motorcycle cop." Photo courtesy of Vector.

The composition of the Vector helmets is a lot different from the military helmets. The helmet has a tough polycarbonate shell over its surface which is used to mushroom or flatten the bullet so that more of a cross-sectional area is created with the projectile. Behind the outer shell of the helmet is a number of layers of soft (non-composite) Kevlar fabric. Because the Kevlar is not in a resin or other material, it is able to deform and more fully contain the bullet, transferring the bullet's energy across a wider area. To prevent blunt trauma to the wearer, the inner vinyl shell of the helmet absorbs the force of impact transferred from the Kevlar. These helmets are available in Level II-A and II protection levels and in a wide range of colors, including white, black, and blue. Price ranges from $150 to $200.

Vector also markets standard police and riot helmets which can be upgraded to ballistic helmets by adding a "ballistic shroud" over the helmets. The shrouds come in a standard model, which looks much like the camouflage cover used on military helmets, or a full-coverage shroud which extends down to the lower neck of the wearer. The shrouds give Level II-A protection to areas covering the helmet and Level I or more protection in areas below the helmet. (These shrouds are not designed to be used with helmets other than those marketed by Vector and may not offer nearly as much protection if used with other helmets.)

Cost of the Vector non-ballistic helmets runs from $60 to $70 (depending on the model). The short Level II-A shroud costs $120, with a Level II-A full shroud costing $195; the Level II full shroud costs $250.

To complete an officer's protection, a riot shield is also available for the Vector helmets. The face shield can also be upgraded to give Level II-A protection. The face shield attaches to the screw holes on the Vector helmets and positively locks into either an open or closed position when in place on the helmet. Cost is $50.

Because of the problems with blunt trauma on the skull, soft armor caps (like the "Command Cap" offered

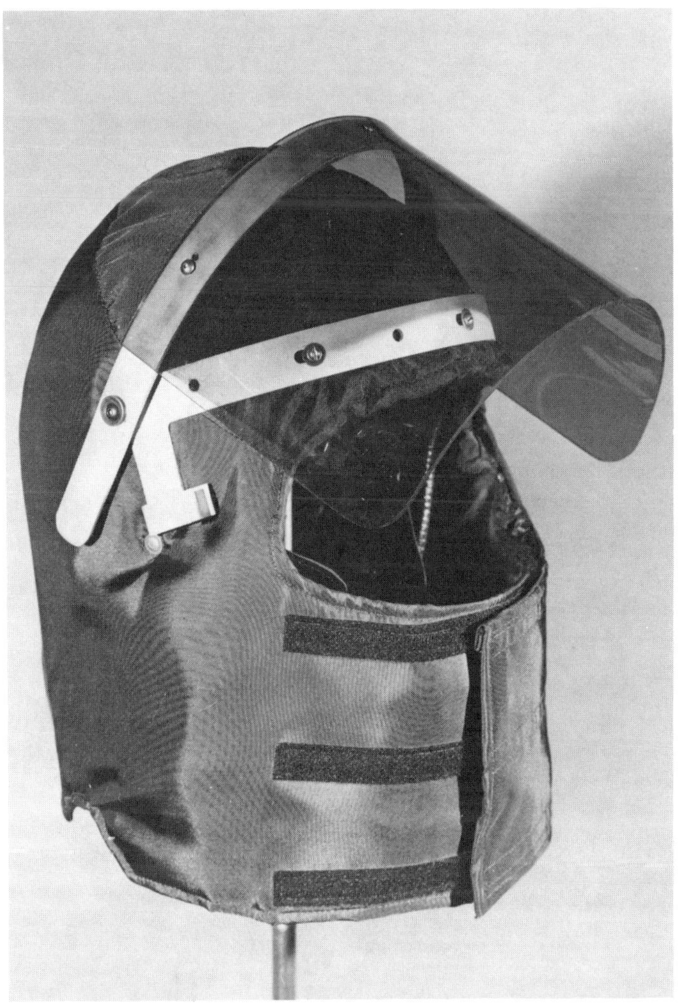

This modern face shield used with helmets can give Level II-A protection and locks in both the open and closed positions when in place on the helmet. Coupled with the ballistic shroud, it would give an officer a high level of head protection. Photo courtesy of Vector.

by Silent Partner for $60) will minimize risk, but not eliminate it completely. A serious head injury will probably result given a "hit" with a large bullet. However, the cap does provide much psychological comfort and is undoubtedly better than nothing at all.

A ballistic shroud can convert a riot helmet into a high-protection piece of head gear. This full-coverage shroud, by Vector, gives Level II-A protection to areas covering the helmet, and Level I or more protection in the areas below the helmet. Photo courtesy of Vector.

Glasses and Goggles

While they don't offer nearly the protection of vests or helmets, new plastics used in glasses and goggles offer a lot of ballistic protection.

The best of these materials is polycarbonate, which is capable of stopping shot pellets fired from a shotgun or bullet fragments created by a ricochet. Polycarbonate is a thermoplastic which—for any given thickness—is six times as strong as glass and, when defeated, doesn't shatter or split. The material is lightweight and clear but has a tendency to scratch easily and could be damaged by water. Therefore, it wasn't used for glasses or goggles until recently when a tough finish was developed which gives a scratch-resistant coating to the lens.

The best-known company producing these glasses is the French firm of Bolle which offers a wide range of sunglasses, shooting glasses, and goggles—any of which give a lot of extra eye protection. (The sunglasses also give almost complete filtration of ultraviolet and infrared light as an added benefit.) Currently, the best supplier of Bolle products (including prescription lenses) in the U.S. is Brigade Quartermasters. Prices for Bolle goggles and sunglasses run from $16 to $80, depending on the model. Prescription lenses cost $150.

Jones Optical also markets a number of styles of glasses and goggles made of the same tough polycarbonate material. The company claims that their combat goggles, which have a three mm-thick lens, were able to stop a .38 Special bullet fired from 15 yards during a test conducted by The Travelers Insurance Company. A similar test conducted by *Soldier of Fortune* magazine had similar results, with the lens remaining intact and showing only deformation and scuffing at the point of impact. Jones Optical glasses cost from $29 to $90, depending on the style, and the "combat specticals" (goggles) cost $30 to $40.

Combat goggles can give the wearer extra protection. Coupled with a ballistic helmet and vest, the wearer is highly immune to low-velocity bullets and shell fragments.

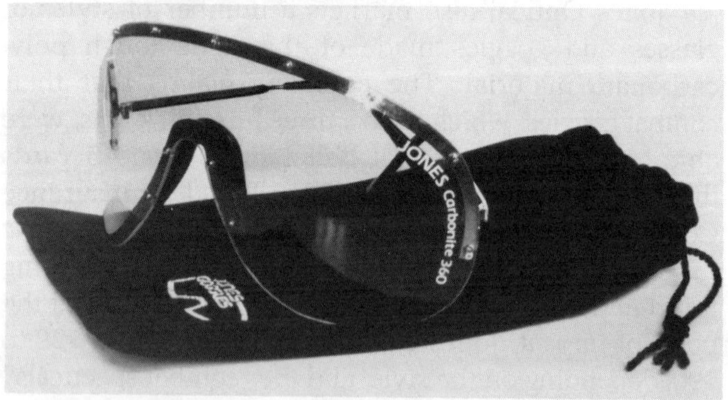

Glasses made of polycarbonate material, while appearing ordinary, may give the wearer an extra edge of protection from low-velocity bullets or shell fragments. Photo courtesy of Jones Optical.

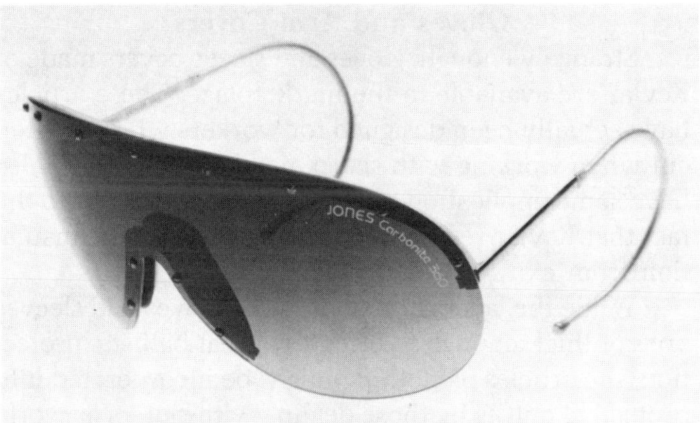

The Jones Optical Company has found that their combat goggles, which have a 3mm-thick lens, are able to stop a 38 Special bullet fired from 15 yards. A similar test conducted by *Soldier of Fortune* magazine had similar results with the lenses remaining intact and showing only deformation and scuffing at the point of impact. Photo courtesy of Jones Optical.

Jones Optical markets a number of designer-style glasses and goggles which are highly resistant to impact. The wearer has an extra margin of safety and style as well. Photo courtesy of Jones Optical.

Gloves and Arm Covers

Strangely enough, gloves and sleeve covers made of Kevlar are available in the marketplace. These articles have actually been designed for workers who are often cut when working with sharp metal or glass. They also have some application to heat protection, thanks to the fact that Kevlar resists burning and offers some insulation from extremely hot objects.

While the layers of Kevlar in the gloves and sleeves are not thick enough to offer any great ballistic protection, the articles of clothing might be incorporated into protective outfits by those dealing with rioters or working in prison-control situations where glass, ice picks, or other sharp weapons might be a consideration. (Japanese riot gear often includes a hard plastic forearm guard which extends from the elbow down over the back of the hand. This armor is designed only for protection against rocks and blows with blunt objects, however, and is not available in the U.S.)

The gloves are made of a terry cloth-like material and look like standard work gloves. Cost is only four dollars per pair. The sleeve covers are double thick and fourteen inches long, with a thumb slot which keeps the sleeve from riding up on the wearer's arm; cost is five dollars. Both are available from Direct Safety Company.

Shields

With the various riots of the 1960s and 1970s the shield has reemerged as a viable piece of armor in the twentieth century. While many of the shields used offer little protection from more than bottles and rocks, some are actually ballistic armor.

Perhaps the most widely used, and the least noticeable, of the ballistic shields are the ballistic clipboards and briefcases. The clipboards are usually made of Kevlar composite and drilled to accept the spring-loaded clip normally found on clipboards. A strap is usually added to the back of the clipboard so that it can be easily used as a shield. Because the clipboard is com-

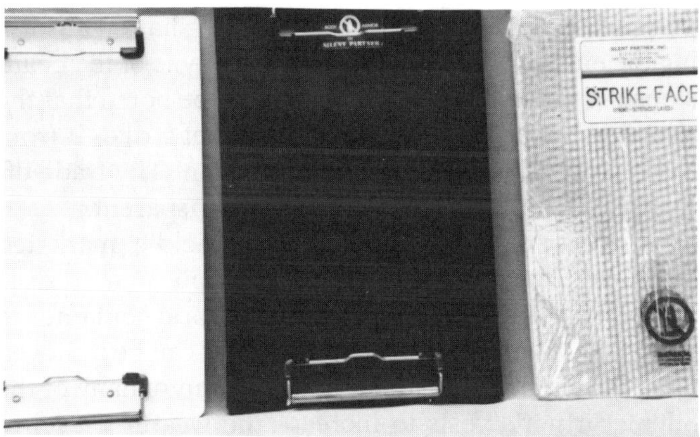

Among the most widely used, and least noticeable, of the ballistic shields are ballistic clipboards. Clipboards are usually made of Kevlar composite or have Kevlar inserts. Often a strap is affixed to the back of the clipboard so that it can be easily used as a shield. Because the armor is commonly used by policemen to carry out their paperwork, it serves a dual purpose when carried and appears very unobtrusive to those who don't realize what it is. Photo courtesy of Silent Partner.

monly used by policemen to carry out their paperwork, it serves a dual purpose when carried and appears very unobtrusive to those who don't realize what it is.

Most briefcases are standard, off-the-shelf briefcases which have a Kevlar composite panel (or occasionally a steel plate) placed in them. These, too, are quite unobtrusive but more suited to use by diplomats, business executives, or bodyguards.

One source offering clipboards, a clipboard with a form holding compartment, and briefcase liners is the William J. Donovan Company. Their armor is created with Kevlar and also uses fiberglass to reinforce the ballistic sheets. A wide range of sizes of case liners and clipboards is available, with both Level I and II-A being available. Costs range from $32 to $50.

Vector offers a clear acrylic clipboard which gives Level II-A protection to an officer behind it. It has a handle and must be pointed at the source of the bullet which is coming toward it. In such a case, the clear polycarbonate surface of the shield will shatter, absorbing the energy of the board while the acrylic of the board stops the bullet. Cost is $50. (It should be noted that the Vector clipboard is "one way." If a bullet strikes it from the rear, it gives less ballistic protection. The trade-off for this inconvenience is that it is transparent.)

Another clipboard shield ("The Shield"), marketed by Silent Partner, uses a hard laminate and flexible Kevlar enclosed in a Cordura nylon fabric container to give protection. Interestingly, the armor can be removed from the clipboard carrier and inserted into many of the Silent Partner's vests to increase the wearer's level of protection.

One interesting camouflage shield is the "Armorbrella," which looks like a black umbrella but has Kevlar incorporated into its fabric. When the owner opens up the umbrella, it creates a shield behind which he can hide. The Armorbrella is available in a Level "I+" and II-A versions for $1,195 and $1,395, respectively. While this shield isn't as cost-effective as a good vest, the Armorbrella might have some use for protecting visiting dignitaries or the like.

Large shields more like those used in ancient times are also available. Designed to protect the user's head and body, these generally give II-A protection and are ideal both for riot control or some types of SWAT operations where the user doesn't know what type of threat he is facing and has minimal possibilities for concealment.

Point Blank offers a shield with a ballistic glass window in it so that the user can see what he's facing without having to peer around the edge of the shield. The shield has a "bicycle grip" handhold with a Velcro-adjustable band for securing the shield to the arm just below the elbow. A Velcro identification badge can also be attached to or quickly removed from the front of the shield.

Vector's "Ballistic Shield" is made of clear Lexan with a polycarbonate coating which shatters upon

Large shields designed to protect the user's head and body are ideal both for riot control and some types of SWAT operations where the user doesn't know what type of threat he is facing. Photo courtesy of Vector.

impact with a projectile, thereby absorbing much of the bullet's energy. The entire shield is transparent except for the padded area where the forearm contacts the shield when it is held. A similar "Riot Shield" is also available from Vector; this shield is *not* capable of offering ballistic protection from most bullets but is ideal for protection from the Molotov cocktails, bottles, and rocks which often accompany a riot.

*

As ballistic armor makes its way to the battlefield along with new chemical/biological equipment, it is possible that the two may be incorporated into protective armor which looks similar to a space suit or outfit worn by storm troopers in *Star Wars*. Yet, even as such armor is being developed, work is being done on armor-piercing rounds which will make the armor obsolete. Only time will tell how much armor will make its way from the designers' drawing boards into the crime-prevention and military marketplace.

4:

Bomb Supression

Ballistic fabrics are especially efficient at stopping low-velocity projectiles, are flexible, and allow some gas to pass through them. This makes them ideal for containing the shrapnel created by small bombs. Therefore, blankets made of ballistic fabric are often used by anti-terrorist units or police bomb squads to deal with potential bombs of unknown origin.

Blast-containing systems are usually created by fabricating ballistic materials into two components: a heavy blanket and a blast-containment ring. In use, the wide ring of fabric is first placed on its edge around the explosive device, and the blanket is then placed over the containment ring and the bomb. The containment ring channels the force of the blast upward, and the blanket flexes and contains most of the fragments created by the explosion. While the gases created by the blast are not contained, most of the bomb fragments are. Consequently, little damage is done other than that created by the blast pressure wave (i.e., broken windows, damaged eardrums, etc.). Containing shrapnel greatly reduces the casualties produced by small bombs.

If a single or dual blanket is used to cover an explosive device without using a containment ring, the

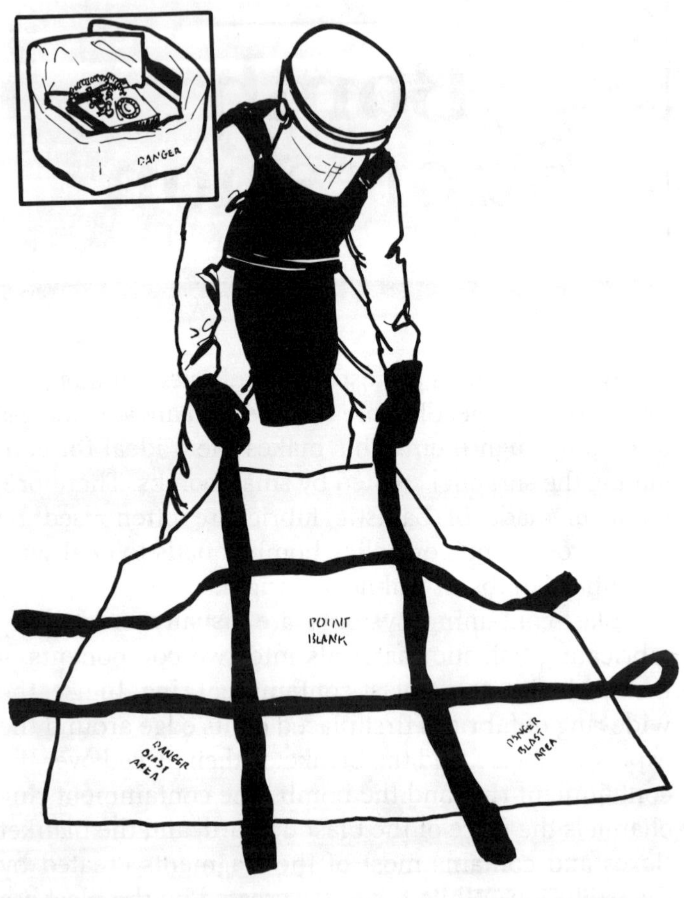

Bomb-containment equipment makes use of a wide ring of fabric placed on its edge around the explosive device coupled with a "blanket" which is placed over the containment ring and the bomb. The containment ring channels the force of the blast upward and the blanket flexes and contains most of the fragments created by the explosion.

blanket must be cut so that its outer edges can drop down to the ground and contain most of the blast shrapnel. If a blanket lacks this type of edge, much of the force of the blast will be directed outward under the edge of the blanket and may cause severe leg and foot injuries to those who have failed to evacuate the area in time.

A ballistic protection rating of Level I or II is generally sufficient to contain the blast of most small bombs, but very large bombs can't be contained by any system currently available. Too, even with a small bomb, there is no guarantee that bomb shrapnel will be contained in a ballistic blanket. It should therefore be remembered that any bomb suppression system is ideally *never* tested. It is a safety device to improve the survival chances of those trying to disarm or move a bomb and for minimizing damage if an explosive device should go off prematurely. Personnel using such a bomb-suppression system must observe all precautions which would be normally followed if the system were not available.

To give some idea of just what could be contained by their bomb-supression systems, Point Blank tested its "Dual Bomb Suppression Blanket" inside a small building equipped with test dummies. It found that its system could contain a twelve- by two-inch pipe bomb charged with three fourths of a pound of smokeless pistol power. It could contain the blast of three sticks of 60 percent dynamite with minimal damage to the building and only slight "injury" to the test dummies in close proximity to the blast. (While this is certainly good, it should be noted that bombs of this size for the most part fall into the "amateur class." With the large bombs often encountered today, some injuries will probably result if only a blanket is being used without other precautions and protective equipment.)

Point Blank has several bomb-suppression systems available. Their bomb-containment rings are made of ballistic nylon with a protective covering to prevent damage to the nylon from ultraviolet light or other environmental conditions. The rings have a Level I rating and are available in both a 6 inch × 4 foot model and a 1 × 6 foot size. The smaller containment ring weighs 4.5 pounds and the larger, 5.9 pounds.

Blankets designed to be used with the rings are also made of ballistic nylon covered with a protective material. Point Blank's 4×4 foot blanket is designed for use with the smaller ring, and a 4×6 foot is available for the larger containment ring. Levels of protection available for both sizes of blankets are Levels I and II. The 4×4 foot blankets weigh 23 pounds for Level I and 45 pounds for Level II; 4×6 blankets are 28 and 54 pounds, respectively.

Point Blank also makes a "double" bomb-suppression blanket. It consists of two 6-foot square blankets of ballistic nylon inside a protective cover. The blankets are connected so that they both are used at once. This double blanket is quicker (and often safer) to use since it need only be draped over a bomb without bothering with the ring containment system. The dual blanket weighs a little less than sixty pounds.

All the Point Blank bomb blankets have canvas straps over them which extend beyond each blanket's edges so that the straps can be used to move and carry the blankets. All models of the blankets can also be constructed with Kevlar upon request. Although Kevlar equipment is more expensive, the resulting equipment weighs less while giving a comparable protection factor.

Bomb-suppression blankets and other equipment should have a printed warning on them which states the equipment is for use over a bomb. Since the bomb may be left under the blanket for some time, there is always an outside possibility that someone might wander into the area without realizing the danger. A large, printed warning may alert them to get out of the area quickly and to leave the blanket and bomb alone. Curiosity has killed more than cats!

Point Blank also makes a small letter-bomb pouch which might be of use to some government agencies or others who risk receiving such dangerous materials through the mail. The pouch weighs 17.6 pounds and measures 17 by 17 inches when closed. When a suspicious letter or small package is received, it can be placed in the pouch and left to be turned over to the proper authorities. Because most "letter bombs" turn out to be false alarms, a letter-bomb pouch can facilitate the clearing of an area and is less apt to create bad relations between organizations (who might otherwise be seen as crying, "Wolf") and bomb-disposal squads.

Any suspicious package or large envelope placed in the pouch is potentially dangerous. Even though the pouch should contain any explosion which might result, don't become cavalier about the dangers just because the danger is in the pouch. There is no guarantee that the explosion would be contained. Treat an explosive in the pouch as if it were out of the pouch.

Protective clothing for personnel working with bombs can be purchased "off the shelf" in the form of ballistic armor. Bomb-disposal squads should wear ballistic vests with groin and neck extension/protective panels as well. Ballistic helmets with ballistic face shields are also necessities. Ideally, clothing worn by the members in the bomb-disposal team would be made of Nomex. (Nomex is another aramid fiber developed by Du Pont. It is highly abrasive-resistant, will not burn, and is very resistant to many dangerous chemicals. At the same time, it breathes and feels quite similar to cotton. A number of military suits—especially those made for pilots—are made of Nomex.)

Because fingers can be blown off when they come in close proximity to an explosion (even when there is no shrapnel), care should be taken to use tools rather than fingers whenever working on or moving explosive devices of unknown origin. In general, the more space that can be maintained between personnel and an explosive, the less severe the wounds will be should the bomb go off. Stay as far away as possible from explosive devices and never "let down" your guard until the device is safely disposed of.

Whatever the type of bomb, it should ideally be moved to a safe area and detonated or otherwise disposed of there. With this in mind, in addition to making bomb-disposal containment rings and blankets, the William J. Donovan Company makes containment bins and transport trailers for use by police bomb squads. These are necessary to minimize damage and injury if the bomb should explode while en route to a safe location.

All bomb-disposal work should be done only by experts and should never be attempted by those who are not highly trained to do the job. Many bombs fail to work and should not be tampered with—they may start working again! Anyone finding a box, unattended bag, etc., should assume it is an explosive device and should spread a warning so that the area is evacuated and the authorities in charge of such work notified. Bomb blankets, containment rings, etc., are not normally purchased by businesses or individuals and should be used only by bomb-disposal experts.

5: Armored Civilian Vehicles

From the times of the "Old West," stage coaches, and later trucks and cars, have been armored against bullets. Most early bullet-resistant endeavors used iron or steel sheets to achieve protection. Therefore excessive weight of the armored vehicles required a sacrifice of speed and the size of the load that could be carried effectively in them.

Steel or titanium armor and thick layers of tempered glass are still in use with armored trucks (sometimes called "armored cars") like those used by Brinks and other courier services. Such vehicles work well provided that high speed, good gas mileage, or a low profile are not important considerations.

When a low profile is needed by dignitaries or the rich and famous, the modern automobile is usually the vehicle of choice. In such a vehicle, heavy steel armor is not ideal because it counters the ability of the car to travel quickly during emergency conditions. Also, with the push toward energy conservation, the large car needed to carry steel armor is highly visible on today's highways.

New composite armor or even soft ballistic nylon and Kevlar are the ideal solutions to such problems and can be used to supply the level of protection needed to those inside a car without increasing the weight limitations by a substantial amount. While the armor created using modern ballistic fibers may cost more than steel-plate armor, it's not prohibitively expensive. And, since most armored vehicles are custom made, composite or soft armor is often actually cheaper to use than steel plate to armor a vehicle; the new plastics are easy to cut and shape and don't require the extensive welding required by steel plate. Thus armor using modern fibers is less expensive than armor comprised of steel plates when labor is taken into account.

Regardless of the type of materials used, armored cars are out of the price range of most people. Currently, prices of armored cars start at around $40,000 and extend well into the hundreds of thousands of dollars. The old cliché "if you have to ask the price you can't afford it" is certainly applicable with armored cars.

Not all of the cost is due to the armor. Some other "options" have to be added to the car both to help support the extra weight of the armor and also because the driver of such a car needs extra capabilities to avoid the potential trouble that creates the need for armor in the first place. Therefore, most armored cars have extra large braking systems, oversized engines, and expensive suspension systems. Often other "James Bond" options such as "run flat" tires, explosion-proof gas tanks, inside/outside intercom, razor-sharp edges under the body to keep rioters from overtuning the car, and even smoke-screen and oil-slick generators are added as well.

Where armament can (legally or otherwise) be carried for self-defense, many armored cars also have firing ports in their armor. These are small areas where there are gaps in the ballistic armor so that those inside the car may fire through the car body. The first few bullets going out of the car will cut through the metal body and thereafter an open area is made for consecutive shots. Cars so equipped usually have hidden compartments in armrests or seats in which to store weapons.

Making the glass of a car bullet-resistant is a lot of work, too, especially if the windows are to roll down. Ideally, the "roll down" windows should be limited to just one or two windows since the extra thickness of the plastic laminate or layers of tempered glass needed to create such a window requires a lot of custom work to get the windows to operate properly. Because windows can't be lowered without defeating protective shielding, armored cars should have adequate air conditioning as well as auxiliary defrosters and deicers to keep the windows clear and closed.

Recently, the NHTSA (National Highway Traffic Safety Administration) decided to allow the use of a removable bullet-resistant plastic shield which can be mounted behind the windshield of a standard car. Since many "counter attacks" against terrorists or would-be assassins can be countered by driving at or over an attacker, these shields make a lot of sense since they can give protection to the driver as he drives headlong at anyone firing at him.

Most armor decreases the engine noise as well as noise coming from traffic outside the car. This is not without its problems since a driver often needs to hear car horns or other warning signals. To overcome this drawback, armored cars often have exterior microphones located on each of their four corners. The sound from these is mixed into an amplifier and then piped to a speaker near the driver (as has been used with many of the limousines used by U.S. Presidents).

Some car companies will armor cars for their customers. Mercedes-Benz, Ford of England, and Saab have all admitted to sometimes doing such work for clients.

Finding other companies to handle such work is not easy. One of the older armored-car makers which handles a lot of such work is Hess & Eisenhardt of Cincinnati. But there are some "new kids" making custom armored cars, now that the new materials are available. One of the larger companies offering such work is Per Mar Security and Research Corporation. Generally, either of these companies will handle any work you may need to have done or can refer you to persons in your area who can do the work.

The possibility of do-it-yourself work also exists since the new materials are readily available. Provided you know how to work on the various body parts of a car and have access to the tools to cut and adapt the ballistic armor to the sizes needed inside the body of the car, the expense involved would be considerably less than hiring a professional company to do the job.

Whoever does such work, it's important to be sure that a lightweight plastic armor is used rather than steel if a small car is being armored. When the armor is assembled, you should also be sure that the armor is overlapped at the seams, and that there are no gaps in the armor at junctions in the car's body or where bolts are used in the body. Lack of overlapping can allow bullets to enter through seams; bolts can become secondary missiles when struck by high-powered bullets.

Ideally the engine will also be armored so that the vehicle can continue to function even if attacked. Given time, almost any defense can be defeated; the idea is not to hang around giving an attacker a chance to do that. Having an engine that can't be damaged early in the attack will assure your ability to escape.

Limited armoring will still give sufficient protection and may keep from digging too deeply into one's wallet. In such a case, armor is placed only on the doors, firewall, and trunk of a car. Since attacks from above or below a car are rare, it's possible to have nearly the same amount of protection for about a tenth of the expense if you're willing to have limited protection and do away with the custom work involved in creating a fully armored car.

Security and maneuverability can also be increased by purchasing a standard car with power steering, power windows (if any open), high-intensity headlights, and locks controlled from the driver's seat. A locking hood and a locking gas cap are essential to prevent tampering with your car. (An electronic security system tends to discourage car theft.) These options all add to one's safety in such a car for very little expense. Coupled with good car tools, flashlight, first-aid kit, etc., the car and occupants should be able to handle many attacks or emergencies.

When picking a car, try to keep the idea of maintaining a low profile. If you have a vehicle that sticks out, it's easier to attack. Therefore, armor a vehicle that will blend into the local traffic. (Also avoid distinctive paint jobs, license tags which spell words, and bumper stickers.)

An armored car doesn't give enough protection if used improperly or if extra chances are taken because of a false feeling of security. Doors should always be locked, routes kept secret, schedules varied, and you should get into and out of the car only in safe areas.

Whatever level of protection you've achieved with your car, the greatest danger you face is having your large investment stolen (rather than attacked by terrorists or the like). Therefore, you must take all precautions not to let your expensively modified car be stolen: Don't leave it unlocked or with the keys in it. Don't park the car and leave it unattended if it's in the open or some public parking area. Always arm the security system before leaving the car.

Before getting into your car, check it out to be sure someone hasn't broken into it, tampered with it, or secured any devices to it. If you don't take the time, you may ruin fingerprints or—worse yet—discover the hard way that a "guest" is in the backseat or that a bomb has been placed in your vehicle. (Spots to check for bombs are the tail pipe, wheel wells, or under the tires. Also, watch for any grease spots, hand prints, or wires which may be where they shouldn't.)

You or your driver should be a little paranoid on the road. The fact alone that one out of ten drivers on the road is probably legally drunk is enough of a reason to drive cautiously. Coupled with the random violence which is often found on the roadway, where short tempers prevail, and the immature are behind the wheel, a little paranoia is good common sense.

You may have to deal with more than just angry motorists. Though incidents of criminals using roadblocks or trying to force people off the road are rare, it's possible and even likely that such may occur if you're concerned about kidnappers or terrorists.

Defensive Driving Tips

If you are a potential target for either group, then you or your driver should enroll in some defensive-driving courses. One organization giving such training is ESI (Executive Security International).

The following behind-the-wheel rules and techniques for avoiding criminals or terrorists are relatively simple but take some work to master:

1. Be alert. If you anticipate trouble, it's easier to avoid. Be aware of what is happening on the road ahead and behind you. Always have a possible "escape route" you can swing into if trouble develops. Everyone in the car should have their seat belts on at all times.

Many times kidnappers have practice runs before they actually carry out the crime; being alert will help you spot them, and varying your schedule helps you thwart them. If you do see suspicious persons or activities, report them to the authorities.

2. If you need to stop in a hurry (because of a roadblock set up by terrorists, for example), the quickest way—if the road surface isn't wet or icy—is to slam on your brakes and hold them down until you're stopped. The car may skid; to get out of this, let up momentarily on the brakes. Otherwise hold them down.

3. Keep your car's engine running and in gear if trouble is anticipated. This allows you to get out of the area quickly or to even use the car as a weapon if you should have to.

If someone tries to get into your car when you've

been forced to stop (or stopped for any other reason such as a stop sign), floor the accelerator and drive off. Don't wait around to see if the person will be successful in their attack on your car. They may be in earnest or they may just be a diversion to allow others to block off your escape. Go forward or backwards, push other cars out of the way, or do whatever will get you away.

4. Learn how to quickly reverse your direction and change your route to avoid any dangers ahead of you. To turn your car around in a hurry to avoid a roadblock, don't use a "U" turn. Instead, use the bootlegger's turn. To execute this turn, back the car up at high speed and cramp the wheel to the side; this will get you through half a turn even on a narrow street. Next, whip the wheel around and head out in the direction you were coming from.

5. Use the weight and power of the car to defeat roadblocks. While the bootlegger's turn is preferable to ramming a roadblock, if a car is blocking you from behind, turning around may not be an option. The secret to getting through a roadblock created with parked cars is in maintaining the car's speed and in aiming for the lightest part of the cars forming the roadblock (the heaviest part of the car is where the motor is and the lightest area is the opposite end). Your speed must bc maintained until your car is well clear of the roadblock.

As most roadblocks are created by placing cars across the road, if you slam into the light end of one or both of the cars in the roadblock, they will actually rotate around their heavier ends and your car will go through in a revolving-door fashion. Because your chances of having the light end of both vehicles together is small, it's usually better to hit just one car if possible even if two are involved in the roadblock. And of the two, ram the lighter car.

If two front-engine cars have been skillfully positioned to create a roadblock by placing them nose to nose across the road, you'll have to either drive off the road around them or aim for the center and hit them at maximum speed. This is the hardest type of roadblock to break through, so avoid doing so if at all possible. If you have a large enough car and enough momentum, it is possible to do so, and both cars in the roadblock should rotate out of the way. Expect to have much damage done to your car.

Don't worry about exploding gas tanks. These are rare in collisions, and occupants of a car whose tank has ruptured usually have enough time to escape it provided they aren't injured. (Wear your seat belt; those who don't in order to escape a burning car usually suffer so many injuries they couldn't escape even if the car should start on fire.)

6. Use the weight of your car and its armor to avoid being forced off the road. By pushing the heaviest part of your car against the lightest area of an opposing car trying to force you off the road, you can actually force the criminal's car to go into a spin which rotates away from your vehicle. By falling back and letting your opponent's car pull up alongside your car, you set the stage for your maneuvering. When the criminal pulls his car toward yours, get the front wheels of your car (assuming this is the heaviest area where your engine is) lined up with the rear wheels of the criminal's car (if the engine on his car is in front). You'll need to either brake quickly or accelerate to do this and then act quickly as he'll realize you're planning something.

Once you've lined the cars up with your front wheels opposite his rear wheels, slam over into your opponent's car; if he's attempting to do the same thing to your car, all the better. As the two cars slam together, accelerate. Your maneuvers will cause your opponent's car to spin out of control and—depending on his driving skills — his car will either go off the road or spin into the ditch on your right. Continue to accelerate so that you'll be clear of him should his car fly out of control or wreck.

If more than one car is trying to force you off the road, the tactics are the same as above but with a little divide-and-conquer thrown in. Avoid any car ahead of you and concentrate on the car beside you. Use the same tactics as outlined above; slam into the car beside you and make it spin. You deal with the cars ahead and behind you as outlined below in the next step.

7. If several cars are trying to box you in, they will probably try to slow down and force you to stop. Don't come to a complete stop because it will be nearly impossible to start moving again once you've lost the momentum of your forward travel and the criminals' cars have locked their brakes. Instead, slam into the rear of the car in front of you before it stops, and push it out of the way. If the car ahead pulls to one side as you push it, you may be able to spin it out of the way. Work to get ahead of the group of cars or out of their trap. If it is impossible to push the car ahead out of the way, consider ramming the car behind you or backing around it and executing a bootlegger's turn. Whatever you do, *do not stop* trying to get away until the car will no longer run. Your life and freedom are at stake.

If armed men get out of the car ahead of you, don't stop for them. Try to hit them; they'll be gone before you get there!

6: Armored Military Vehicles

Increasingly air and land vehicles are getting more sophisticated and closer to the action; concurrently anti-vehicular artillery is advancing to cope with this new menace. Though modern vehicles may certainly be much more maneuverable and thus able to escape harm's way more quickly than those of a decade ago, their increased usage in the vicinity of battle requires that they be as invulnerable as possible. Towards this end is the ongoing research and application of armor for military vehicles.

Military Aircraft Armor

With an aircraft, where weight limitations are important and where large-caliber, high cyclic-rate weapons fire at it, adequate armor is an impossibility.

However, some armor is found on aircraft to protect the pilot and engines from flak, small-arms fire, or bullet fragments from large bullets hitting elsewhere on the aircraft. Interestingly, some armor is also being added to aircraft in the form of ballistic composites which replace what was originally non-ballistic molded plastic or even metal. Thus, seats, helmets, panels, insulation, and the outer body could or are being made of Kevlar composites to reduce the risk to the pilot, crew, and instruments. In addition to the added protection offered by composites, the armor gives the added benefit of reducing the aircraft's overall weight.

This armor is important because without it, the complexity of modern aircraft—especially helicopters—can make them very vulnerable to small-arms fire. As an example of this, consider the fact that the United States lost nearly one third of all the helicopters fielded in Vietnam. While some of these losses were caused by pilot error or sabotage on the ground, many losses were caused by enemy small-arms fire. Likewise, a U.S. helicopter was recently brought down by a kid who made a "lucky" shot with a .22 rifle and hit a tail rotor, and a newsman recently reported a similar shot made by an Afghan rebel using an AK-74!

Because of their vulnerability, helicopters have in the past tried to minimize the time they present themselves as targets. When close to the ground, their tactics involved popping up and firing rockets or machine guns and then quickly hiding behind cover so that returned fire doesn't hit them. (However, this was not a hard-and-fast rule, and if a pilot thought that there was no heavy weapons in the group he was attacking, he might hang in place or circle an area while the aircraft's gunners saturated it with fire. The helicopter scene in the United Artist 1979 movie, *Apocalypse Now*, gives a good idea of how helicopters can operate when there is little effective ground fire.)

A helicopter is especially vulnerable to small-arms fire in several areas: the tail rotor, the turbine air intakes, and—on many Russian choppers—at the oil intake that's conveniently located under the red star on its fuselage. New composites are doing away with much of this danger; many helicopters are having their blades made of composite "armor" materials so that the blades have extra strength, are lightweight, *and* are able to survive ground fire and shrapnel hits. In effect, the blades are *all* armor.

Jet fighter planes are less vulnerable to damage with

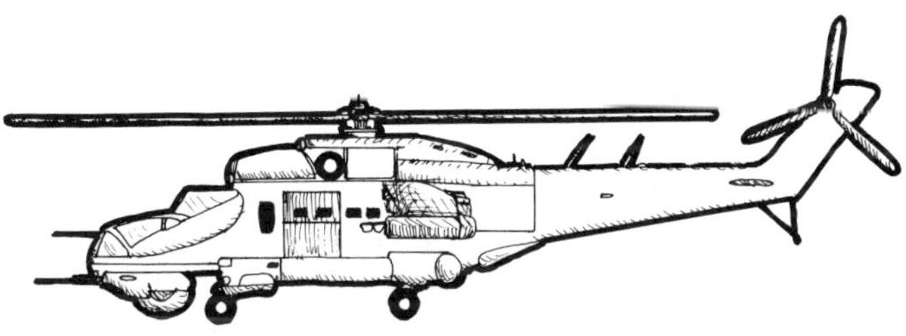

USSR's Hind "D" helicopter can carry eight fully equipped ground troops and has a chin turret with a four-barrel 12.7mm gun or 23mm cannon, four 57mm rocket posts, and four ATGMs (air-to-ground missiles). Nevertheless, insufficient armor allowed an Afghan rebel to shoot down a helicopter similar to this one with a rifle!

small-arms fire because their speed makes them hard to hit with small arms. Also, in combat, jet fighters either maintain a safe altitude or stay close to the ground and pop up to acquire a target. Following the first pass, perhaps during which the plane uses a volley of fire against targets of opportunity, a jet usually will maneuver and return from the opposite direction of the previous attack and use its cannon or machine guns on the second pass. Large bombs may also be released if a major target is spotted by the pilot.

In effect, a jet has used speed and firepower to make up for its need for armor. This appears to be the trend for jets on into the future. While presently the time a jet fighter can keep a target on the ground in its sights is quite short, the time may soon be greatly extended. The weapons on a fighter jet are stationary and the pilot must aim the whole aircraft to hit his target; jet planes can only fire in the direction the nose of the plane is pointed. Researchers are now seriously proposing jet planes with on-board computers which will stabilize the plane to the point that a pilot can turn it sideways in flight to "cover" a target as the fighter goes by it. Coupled with hovering techniques created by redirecting the jet engine exhaust, fighter planes may become extremely formidable to ground troops and other aircraft in the near future.

As the amount of armor on helicopters increases and the maneuverability and fire power of fixed-wing aircraft increases, infantry troops may no longer be trained to use massed small-arms fire to engage aircraft.

The technique of using massed fire to engage aircraft dates back to World War II when Soviet soldiers discovered its effectiveness. There are two ways to deliver this fire. One technique is for all the troops to pick a point ahead of the aircraft and saturate the spot with fire until the aircraft flies into the area. The other way is to gain a proper lead ahead of the aircraft and follow it as it flies by. The first has a guaranteed hit and the second gets the greatest number of multiple hits *if* the group has the correct lead. Because the bullets fired into the air in this manner come back down somewhere, this technique can cause a lot of friendly casualties if care isn't taken. Rifle bullets travel for miles and remain lethal over their entire range so it's easy for a group of troops blazing away at a plane to be killing comrades miles away.

Because a pilot quickly becomes aware of the fact that small-arms fire is hitting his aircraft and because it takes a large number of ground troops to put up an effective barrage of fire, it doesn't take much guesswork to locate the ground forces. When this happens, the pilot may make short work of the troops or call in help to do so. As the armor and/or firepower of planes increases, the wisdom of engaging an aircraft with small arms decreases.

But small portable weapons are being developed which can be used to engage aircraft. Thus the cycle of weapons versus armor is starting another circle. Even as aircraft become less vulnerable to small-arms fire, it seems probable that new weapons may be developed to overcome their free rein on the battlefield.

Tanks and Armored Personnel Carriers

Ground vehicles, because they are not restricted to the weight limitations of aircraft, are where armor reaches its maximum thickness.

Tanks were introduced to battle in World War I and have had a shaky life ever since as the tactics of battle change and designers try to strike a balance between mobility and adequate armor. Currently, the cannons and machine guns mounted on tanks make up about one-third of a mechanized army's ground-based firepower. Because of their armament and armor, modern tanks weigh forty to sixty tons and must move on tracks.

Tanks usually have a covey of foot soldiers along with them. While most people think that these troops are with the tank in order to be protected by it, they

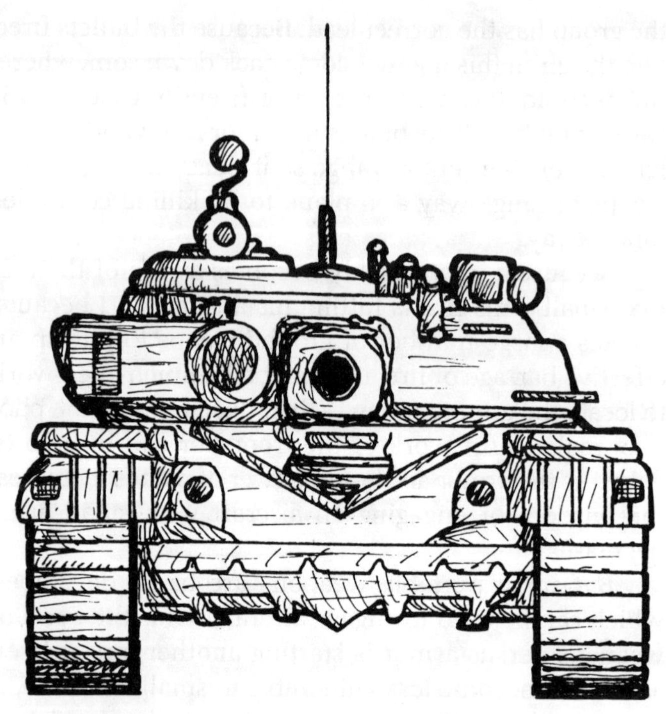

Tanks, introduced to battle in World War I, make up about one-third of a mechanized army's ground-based firepower. Because of their armament and armor, modern tanks weigh 40 to 60 tons and must move on tracks. This USSR T-72 Tank weighs 41 metric tons.

are in fact there to protect the tank from small-arms fire and anti-tank weapons. Additionally, tanks (especially Soviet tanks) usually travel in groups so as to offer fire support for each other.

There are a number of reasons that tanks need all this extra help.

One is that the viewports and periscopes on tanks have to be very small so that they present only minimal targets; if they were large enough to give the tank crew adequate vision, the viewports could be defeated by repeated hits from small-arms fire. The trade-off is that tank personnel have a hard time seeing enemy foot soldiers and the tank often blunders about on the battlefield unless the tank commander is willing to risk looking out his open hatch during battle. (Soviet tanks are especially poor in this area. Because of the placement of view ports, the crew can't even see a soldier within ten meters of them without looking out a hatch, and the main cannon can decapitate the driver if he has had his head out the hatch and isn't being alert.)

While the armor on tanks is quite strong, tanks,like most armor systems, also have some "soft spots" where foot soldiers can disable them if they have the chance to approach the tank and "work" on it without hindrance. Though most designers try to minimize these areas, there are still generally a few that exist. (Again, Soviet tanks are good examples of poor design. Most models have large auxiliary fuel tanks which may create a fire hazard it they aren't jettisoned before battle. It is apparently sometimes possible to set off a Soviet tank's ammo by firing down on it through the air vents on its top.) And when crew members in the tank are trying to cool off or see better through an open hatch, they make excellent targets or leave an opening that hand grenades might be lobbed through with disastrous results.

Finally, the armor on tanks makes it hard to use the weapons mounted in them. Some tanks can't decline their main guns to hit targets within 20 meters of the tank. (Once someone gets to within 20 meters of a Soviet tank, they're safe from both the tank's heavy cannon as well as its coaxially-mounted machine gun.)

So modern tanks need infantrymen along with them to keep enemy foot soldiers away.

Because the modern battlefield could become very toxic due to the use of nuclear, chemical, or biological weapons and because of the speed a modern tank can maintain, troops are currently moved about a lot in APCs (Armored Personnel Carriers, also sometimes called IFVs or Infantry Fighting Vehicles).

These vehicles date back to the half tracks of World War II when some work was done with armored troop carriers. The modern APC has to be armored in order to keep an enemy from attacking the troops in the APC and then taking on the tank without the foot soldiers needed to support it. Because the troops need to see in order to protect the tank (and themselves), most APCs have ports down both their sides so that the troops (usually 7 to 12) can see what's going on on all sides and deliver fire from their rifles through firing ports if they need to do so. Large doors at the rear of the APCs allow the troops to exit in a hurry to protect themselves, their APC, and the tank that's with them. APCs also generally have a large machine gun or even a small cannon mounted on them. These are normally fired by the crew operating the vehicle. Many APCs have tracks like tanks or have a number of wheels to maneuver more easily in heavy mud.

Currently, APCs are becoming *the* target on the battlefield because they have thinner armor than tanks and the troops in them must be dealt with in order to make the tank with them more vulnerable. In an effort to cope with this problem, designers are making APCs more armored and tank-like all the time. Tactics are also being formulated to minimize the risk to troops from anti-tank weapons. The troops in APCs usually "dismount" at the first sign of danger.

As their armor increases and tactics change, APCs

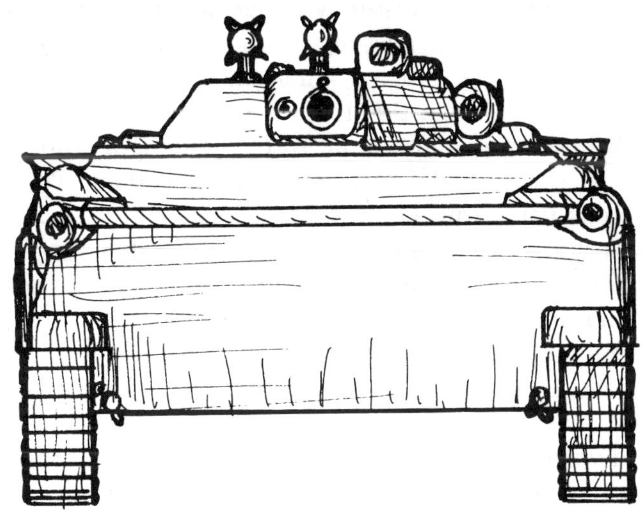

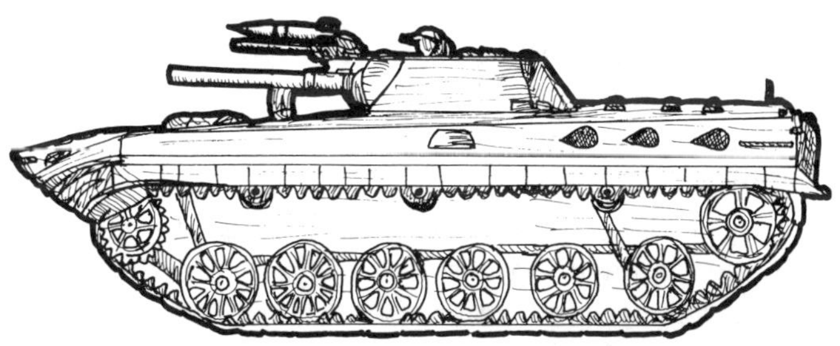

Because the increased potential for lethality found on the modern battlefield and the speed of a modern tank, troops are moved about much of the time in APCs like the Soviet BMP. It normally has a crew of three and carries eight foot soldiers. It has four firing ports on each side and one in the rear door for the troops to use with their rifles as well as a 73mm smoothbore HEAT (high-explosive antitank) cannon, ATGMs, and a 7.62mm coaxial machine gun.

are more able to operate by themselves and are increasingly used either as fast-moving, armored troop transports or with fewer passengers and more equipment, as reconnaissance vehicles. Where these trends will lead is hard to predict at this time.

Whether on a tank or an APC, there are a number of ways to actually defeat the armor used on them. These methods vary from crude to high-tech.

Perhaps the crudest, yet still workable, is the Molotov cocktail. This device can damage most tank engines and will sometimes cause enough problems to drive a tank crew out of the tank. Once they are outside the armor of the tank, they are very vulnerable.

A Molotov cocktail is a small-necked beverage bottle, filled with gasoline (and ideally a thickening agent like Styrofoam or soap), with a rag crammed into the opening, where the rag acts like a wick. Just before using the Molotov, the wick is lit and the Molotov thrown at the intended target. When the Molotov hits the tank, APC, or whatever, it shatters, coating the tank with a film of gasoline. The wick ignites the fumes of the gasoline almost instantly, and a very fearsome fire erupts.

Another rather crude method of destroying a tank is to use a satchel charge placed on the top of the tank.

But these and similar methods of knocking out tanks all require that soldiers must first overcome the foot soldiers guarding the tank and then get near to the tank to do the damage. That's not easy to do. So other weapons have been, and are being, developed to deal with a tank or APC from a greater distance.

And there's a lot of armor on a tank to deal with.

Most tanks now in service use steel for armor. These tanks have up to 14 to 18 inches homogenous steel armor. This armor acts like much thicker armor because of the curved, slanted shapes of the plates, which means that most projectiles hitting the armor actually have to travel up to 28 inches of the steel in order to defeat it.

New composition armor is currently being designed to resist new anti-tank weapons which defeat conventional steel armor. Often called Chobham armor, this composition armor can give excellent results but is presently much more expensive than steel plate. The armor is made up of various layers of ceramics, ballistic nylon, and/or Kevlar (with various combinations and arrangements being held secret by the makers of the armor). The U.S. M1, West German Leopard II, English Chieftain, and Soviet T-80 tanks are all believed to use composite armor to increase their ability to survive on the battlefield. (Because the tactical neutron bomb overcomes the advantages of steel plate in protecting tank crews from radiation, the need for steel plate to protect tank crews on the nuclear battlefield is not much of a consideration.)

The biggest savings with composite armor is in the weight of the armor. Composite armor on a modern tank can give it 60 percent more armor without adding any weight to the design (it will add bulk, of course).

Additionally, tanks "augment" their armor through the use of natural cover whenever possible. If a position is to be held, a tank can "dig in" and use dirt for added protection or prepare to fire at an enemy from over a hill from a defilade position. Coupled with camouflage, a seasoned tank crew can avoid ever having to face an anti-tank weapon.

There are a number of larger weapons systems capable of overcoming the armor of a tank. These include large artillery, ATGMs (Anti-Tank Guided Missiles), self-guided missiles, bombs, and land mines which are all successful in varying degrees against tanks. Probably the most successful weapon to use against a tank is another tank. With this in mind, new tank ammunition is constantly being developed to overcome tank armor. Among the most successful of these thus far are new HESH (High Explosive Squash Head), also called HEP (High Explosive Plastic) shells. These are non-explosive projectiles which transfer their energy into and through the armor of a tank by flattening against it. When this energy is suddenly released, the armor may spall on the inside or shake things lose with great violence so that tank crews are often killed by flying secondary projectiles inside the tank. The principal advantages of the HESH are that it can easily be fired from a tank's cannon and maintains its accuracy over long ranges; this makes it ideal for use by a tank to fight other tanks or APCs.

There are basically two methods of defeating armor. One is to use kinetic energy to break through the armor and the other is to direct explosive energy (or shaped charges) through it.

Kinetic energy uses the energy created by a fast-moving projectile to knock a hole in armor. With current methods of firing projectiles, this requires a very large-caliber weapon to overcome armor as thick as the tank's. (This may change in the near future as work progresses on the "rail gun." This device creates a magnetic charge which propels a projectile at speeds hundreds of times greater than is possible using current smokeless powders or rockets. Such speed would give the energy needed by a relatively small projectile to breach the armor of a tank.)

One type of weapon which can be quite small and carried by foot soldiers is the HEAT (High Explosive, Anti-Tank) weapon. The advantages of these are that they are lightweight and relatively inexpensive. Most are rocket propelled.

The concept of shaped charges dates back to the 1880s when it was discovered that new smokeless powders could create patterns on metal when exploded near them. Work was done to create larger, deeper patterns, and a German scientist named Neumann discovered that if a cone of metal were made and covered with explosive, it was possible to blow a hole through heavy steel plate beneath the cone. By the 1920s and 1930s, the basic cone shape needed to create the most damage became well known, and in 1938 the Swiss were marketing a rifle grenade based on this concept. Soon other countries were creating their own versions of shaped charges delivered as rifle grenades or on the ends of rockets. The war on tanks by foot soldiers began in earnest.

When a HEAT weapon hits an armor plate, its nose flattens against the armor so that the open end of the cone is against the armor. At the same time, the explosive in the HEAT warhead is ignited. The explosion is channeled into the cone-shaped depression in the warhead's nose, and the metal forming the inside of the cone is compressed into a thin wire of metal that is forced into the armor as a metal jet. If the shaped charge is large enough and/or the armor thin enough, this jet of metal will force its way through the armor. When this jet hits the air, the sudden release of pressure turns to heat and the metal vaporizes and showers the area on the other side of the shaped charge with molten metal. If any of the explosive pressure is left over from the HEAT warhead, that too is suddenly released through the tiny opening created by the metal jet. Both the jet of metal and the blast can do grave damage to personnel and equipment behind the armor.

In order for a HEAT weapon to be effective, it must have enough energy to penetrate the armor with its jet of metal. To do this, especially on the thick front armor of a tank, it must also hit the armor plate at a right angle. Given the low profile and curved armor of modern tanks, this is not easy for a foot soldier to do in the heat of battle.

And those designing tank armor are doing all they can to make HEAT weapons ineffective. As mentioned above, in order to avoid the damage done to armor by shaped charges, some armor is now being made of composite materials in a series of layers. Other variations of this type of armor are created with a "sandwich" of steel plates with air spaces or plastic between various layers of steel, with metal "honey combs," or by adding another layer of material over existing steel or composite armor. Any of these has the effect of placing a thin metal shell over the outside of the armor; when a HEAT charge explodes on this shell, the jet from the cone loses energy when dropping into the space between steel layers and is easily deflected by the remaining armor.

Any of these methods can degrade the normal effectiveness of a HEAT warhead down to one-third its normal penetrative powers. Experimental work is also being done with "active" armor which explodes when hit to deflect or ruin a shaped charged before it can cut through armor.

Of course weapons designers are trying to improve their product, too. Work is being done on using multiple shaped charges, one behind the other, to cut through armor. Work is also being done on using lighter metals for the cone lining of the shaped charge; metals like aluminum and magnesium will accelerate the rate at which the jet can cut through metal and create more heat and flash when they finally get through the armor.

Currently, the race between armor and armament is being won by the armor, at least as far as HEAT weapons are concerned. Because the ratio of metal cut is proportional to the diameter of the shaped charge, in order to get through the metal used on the front of a tank (where the armor is thickest) a shaped charge has to be at least seven inches in diameter. This creates a weapon that is not practical to carry on foot. Consequently, most man-portable anti-tank weapons using shaped charges are capable only of defeating armor on the sides or rear of tanks and then only if the shaped charge hits straight on so it travels through the minimum amount of armor.

To make things even worse for anyone fighting a tank with a HEAT weapon, the range of the HEAT projectile is very short, especially when compared to the guns on most tanks and APCs. Therefore, the current strategy for those using HEAT weapons is based on hiding until the tank or APC is alongside or just past you and keeping your fingers crossed.

Nevertheless, there are a number of portable weapons which can be used against parts of tanks in which there is a minimum of armor, and most countries currently are fielding one or more such weapons. (Perhaps one of the most promising of these is a hand grenade developed by the East Germans and modeled after an old World War II Soviet design, since "borrowed" by Western manufacturers. While the advertising for this HEAT grenade shows it blowing a tank apart, the effectiveness—if a soldier could get that close to a tank—is doubtful. It might be of use to a saboteur or against lightly armored vehicles, however.)

Most HEAT weapons are recoilless in that they use a rocket to do the work of getting the warhead to the target. A rocket minimizes the weight of an anti-tank weapon but also creates a complex ballistic arc and a back blast that can often be seen by those in the tank or APC. HEAT weapons are better than nothing, however, and are capable of debilitating a tank or APC provided the infantryman has proper training and luck.

Despite all the threats to the tank, it currently rules the battlefield in much the same way that early knights reigned. But new technology is developing new ways to defeat the tank's armor. Will the tank be displaced by the foot soldier carrying a portable weapon capable of defeating its armor? The knight certainly was . . .

LIGHT ANTI-ARMOR WEAPONS

Weapon	Warhead Diameter (inches)	Length (inches)	Weight (lbs.)	Range (yards)	Armor Penetration (inches)
APILAS	4.3	51	19.5	430	27.6
AT4	3.3	39.3	13	325	15.7
LAW-M72A2	2.6	35.1	5.1	325	12
LAW-80	3.7	59	21	520	23.6
RPG-7	3.3	37	22	430	12.9
RPG-16	2.3	43	28	650	14.8
RPG-18	2.5	41.3	8.8	220	11.8
"Viper"	2.7	46	8	325	15.7

Appendix:

Manufacturers, Dealers and Distributors

Alco Wholesale
16462 Gothard St., Unit E
Huntington Beach, CA 92647
(714) 842-7221
Ballistic vests

Almac Plastics, Inc.
101-10 Foster Ave.
Brooklyn, NY 11236
(718) 257-4444
Lucite, Plexiglas, and bullet-resistant, custom installations

American Acrylic Corp.
400 Sheffield Ave.
West Babylon, NY 11704
(516) 422-2200
Soft and composite armor and materials

American Body Armor & Equipment, Inc.
135 N. New York Ave.
Halesite, NY 11743
(516) 271-0019
Ballistic vests, bomb-handling equipment, etc.

American Police Products
Box 1115
Cape Canaveral, FL 32920
(305) 783-6809
Ballistic vests

Armour of America
P.O. Box 1405
Beverly Hills, CA 90213
(213) 532-0690
Ballistic vests

Armour Wear, Inc.
P.O. Box 62
343 Pecks Rd.
Pittsfield, MA 01201
Protective clothing

Bill Bear, Co., Inc.
Body Armor Division
Box 573
San Marcos, CA 92069
(619) 744-0404
Soft body armor

Brigade Quartermasters, Ltd.
266 Roswell St.
Marietta, GA 30060
(404) 428-1234
Bolle polycarbonate glasses and goggles

Burlington Industrial Fabrics Company
261 Madison Ave.
New York, NY 10016
(212) 953-1100
Kevlar 29 fabric

Burlington Industrial Fabrics Company
1345 Avenue of the Americas
New York, NY 10019
(212) 621-1107
Kevlar 49 fabric

Central Police Supply Co.
1410 Washington Ave.
Houston, TX 77002
(713) 225-4392
Ballistic vests

Chicago Bullet Proof Equipment Co.
2250 Western Ave.
Park Forest, IL 60466
(312) 481-3400
Armor plating

Composite Technologies
2401 Elliot Ave.
Troy, MI 48083
(313) 585-6240
Composite armor

Direct Safety Company
7815 South 46th St.
Phoenix, AZ 85040
(602) 968-7009
Kevlar gloves and sleeves

Du Pont Company
N2522-2 MCD
Wilmington, DE 19898
(302) 774-6485
Kevlar

Executive Armoring Co.
4836 Whirlwind
San Antonio, TX 78217
(512) 654-3905
Custom armor-plating, ballistic vests, etc.

Executive Security International
520 E. Cooper, Ste. 205
Aspen, CO 81611
(303) 920-2323
Training of security personnel and executives on evasive driving, bomb disposal, etc.

General Electric Co., Plastics Group
One Plastics Ave.
Pittsfield, MA 01201
(800) 845-0600
Shatter-proof plastics, etc.

Hess and Eisenhardt
8959 Blue Ash Rd.
Cincinnati, OH 45242
(513) 791-5700
Custom armored-car work

Hi-Pro-Form-Fabrics, Inc.
962 Devon Dr.
Newark, DE 19711
(302) 368-0405
Kevlar fabrics

Jones Optical Company
P.O. Box 3096
Boulder, CO 80307
(303) 447-8727
Polycarbonate glasses and goggles

North American Ordnance Corp.
2271 Star Court
P.O. Box 4288
Pontiac, MI 48057
(313) 852-8735
Ballistic vests

Per Mar Security and Research Corporation
Box 4227
Davenport, IA 52808
(319) 326-6291
Custom armoring of cars

Point Blank
55 Saint Mary's Place
Freeport, NY 11520
(516) 223-4044
Ballistic vests, composite armor, etc.

Porta-King Building Systems
4133 Shorline Dr.
Earth City, MO 63045
(800) 325-1866
Custom bullet-resistant buildings

PPAA (Personal Protective Armor Association)
3200 Greenknoll Rd.
Baltimore, MD 21207
Sets guidelines for classification, sales, and advertising of ballistic vests

Protective Materials Co., Inc.
Folly Mill Rd.
Seabrook, NH 03874
(603) 474-5523
Ballistic armor, bomb-handling equipment, etc.

Second Chance Body Armor, Inc.
P.O. Box 578
Central Lake, MI 49622
(616) 544-5721
Ballistic armor

Sherwood International
18714 Parthenia St.
Northridge, CA 91324
(818) 349-7600
Israeli ballistic helmet

Silent Partner, Inc.
612-18 Third St.
Gretna, LA 70053
(504) 366-4851
Ballistic vests, body armor, etc.

Valley Plastics Supplies, Inc.
7432 N. Fowler Ave.
Clovis, CA 92612
(209) 299-2324
Ballistic fabrics

Vector
921 Broadus St.
Sturgis, MI 49091
(616) 651-3278
Ballistic armor, helmets, shields, etc.

Vehicle Systems Development Corp.
1271 W. 9th St.
Upland, CA 91786
(714) 981-3236
Custom armor-plating

William J. Donovan Company
5 Melrose Court
Hamden, CT 06518
(203) 288-6898
Bomb-handling equipment, ballistic armor, etc.